GREG

Hope

CW00556552

The
Twelve Steps
of Recovery

Success in Recovery Through
a Faith-Based Journey

Dedication

The Twelve Steps of Recovery: Success in Recovery Through a Faith-Based Journey is dedicated to all those seeking success in recovery from any addiction or any struggle of life. May you find true freedom through a faith-based journey of The Twelve Steps of Recovery that ultimately leads you to the loving, caring, and compassionate God of the Bible.

Table of Contents

Acknowledgements

The Twelve Steps of Recovery: Success in Recovery Through a Faith-Based Journey is based on a series of podcast episodes from my podcast, called *The Hope Recovery Podcast,* that present an episode on each of The Twelve Steps of Recovery from a faith-based perspective. While the content in this book is based on many of the same foundational principles of the original podcast episodes, it is revised and expanded in various ways.

The Twelve Steps of Recovery: Success in Recovery Through a Faith-Based Journey is planned to be available in multiple editions.

Regular Edition (5.00 x 8.00)
Large Print Edition (6.00 x 9.00)
Kindle / eBook Edition

The
Twelve Steps
of Recovery

Success in Recovery Through a Faith-Based Journey

Introduction

Welcome to *The Twelve Steps of Recovery: Success in Recovery Through a Faith-Based Journey.* Thank you so much for starting this brand-new journey of recovery and of faith as this book looks at The Twelve Steps of Recovery in a fresh new way with a blend of recovery principles and a biblical faith-based perspective of The Twelve Steps. The Twelve Steps of Recovery, as presented by Alcoholics Anonymous and Narcotics Anonymous, have helped many millions of people to be successful in recovery and one reason they are so successful is because they both encourage people to seek a spiritual experience with God. *The Twelve Steps of Recovery: Success in Recovery Through a Faith-Based Journey* expands on this spiritual and faith-based perspective for each of The Twelve Steps of Recovery.

Regardless of where you are at in your recovery or in your faith, I encourage you to be open to the message of recovery and of faith as presented in *The Twelve Steps of Recovery: Success in Recovery Through a Faith-Based Journey*. It doesn't matter how long you are in recovery, whether days, weeks, months, or years, and it doesn't matter where you are at in your faith or what you may or may not believe about God. My goal with this book is to help you be successful in recovery and to encourage you to consider the role of faith in your recovery. A brand-new life is possible, and it all starts with first being successful in recovery.

The books of *Alcoholics Anonymous* and *Narcotics Anonymous* are the two main recovery fellowships and both present versions of The Twelve Steps. It is clear from the plain reading of The Twelve Steps from each fellowship that they both indicate the importance of a spiritual component of recovery and that a restored relationship with God is key to recovery and even to a brand-new life as well. As you read through this book, I encourage you to look at recovery in a fresh new way and I encourage you to not minimize or dismiss the role of faith in your recovery or in your life.

It is my hope and prayer that this book would help you be successful in recovery and grow in your faith. Success in recovery is absolutely possible when you bring God into your life.

The Twelve Steps:
A Spiritual Foundation

"For faith in a Power greater than ourselves, and miraculous demonstrations of that power in human lives, are facts as old as man himself. We finally saw that faith in some kind of God was a part of our make-up, just as much as the feeling we have for a friend. Sometimes we had to search fearlessly, but He was there."[1]
(Alcoholics Anonymous)

===================================

"But you, Lord, are a compassionate and gracious God, slow to anger, abounding in love and faithfulness.
(Psalm 86:15 NIV)

===================================

"There is a God in heaven; and he is a loving, caring, and compassionate God who wants to help you."[2]
(The Hope Recovery Devotional)

===================================

In this chapter I will look at The Twelve Steps of Recovery and the spiritual foundation of The Twelve Steps. In many ways this is an introduction to The Twelve Steps and the spiritual connection to The Twelve Steps. The Twelve Steps of Recovery were truly a revolutionary approach to recovery. It really was a brand-new approach or strategy to help people gain freedom from the terrible bondage of alcoholism. Eventually, The Twelve Steps were utilized by other recovery groups as well to address many other addictions. The Twelve Steps of Recovery started in 1935 with a very modest and humble beginning by the founders, most commonly known as Bill W and Dr. Bob, and what they started eventually became a world-wide fellowship of recovery. The Twelve Steps had finally given true hope to many people to not only be free from the bondage of alcoholism, but to actually live a full and abundant life without alcohol.

The Twelve Steps of Recovery are made up of action steps if you will. These Twelve Steps are to be performed in sequential order as they build upon each other, ultimately leading you, not only to sobriety, but to a "spiritual experience with God." The Twelve Steps are the foundational action steps or principles used by the two main recovery fellowships, namely Alcoholics Anonymous and Narcotics Anonymous, often referred to as just AA and NA. Alcoholics Anonymous is the largest of the Twelve Step fellowships and the second largest is Narcotics Anonymous, which was founded in 1953. NA uses a slightly different version of the Twelve Steps of Recovery from the AA version, but in my view they really are identical. The NA book speaks about their connection to The Twelve Steps of AA when they say this in the introduction of their book:

> "The Twelve Steps of Narcotics Anonymous, as adapted from A.A., are the basis of our recovery program. We have only broadened their perspective. We follow the same path with a single exception; our identification as addicts is all-inclusive with respect to any mood-changing, mind-altering substance."[3]

The Twelve Steps of Recovery, from AA and NA, have helped millions of people be successful in recovery. Millions of people are now successfully living a life in recovery, with the principles of The Twelve Steps of Recovery. While there are some that prefer other types of support groups that are not Twelve Step related it is clear that The Twelve Steps of Recovery have indeed helped many millions of people be successful in recovery and likely they can help you as well.

As I look at The Twelve Steps of Recovery to me they are very much about God and about having a spiritual experience with God. In the actual wording of the AA Twelve Steps the word "God" is used 4 times and words that refer to God another 5 times. Yes, The Twelve Steps of Recovery are very much about God.

The Twelve Steps are included in the main book of AA, which is also known as the "*Big Book*", and God is referenced throughout the book many times. In addition, the *Big Book* of AA will often refer to God in multiple ways, often as either "the God of your understanding", or as "your higher power" or even just as "God". These terms, while somewhat generic, present God and a spiritual experience with God, in a very welcoming and open manner such that many people find this approach to God a more inviting and a sort-of "neutral" place to start in a spiritual journey to find God. For me, I think this was such a wise decision by the AA founders, because it is a very broad and welcoming statement that encourages people to consider finding God in a fresh, new way. But it still encourages people to seek to find God, and really that is the most important thing, to genuinely seek to find God. Wording like this does not connect AA to any particular faith, or church or denomination, but absolutely brings God into the conversation of recovery and into The Twelve Steps of Recovery and into the decisions of recovery as well. And with this wording, The Twelve Steps do it in a very open and welcoming way.

To this idea of "God" and finding God, Bill W. in the *Big Book* of AA says this from page 12:

"My friend suggested what then seemed a novel idea. He said, "Why don't you choose your own conception of God?" That statement hit me hard. (and later...) It was only a matter of being willing to believe in a Power greater than myself. Nothing more was required of me to make my beginning. I saw that growth could start from that point. Upon a foundation of complete willingness I might build

7

what I saw in my friend. Would I have it? Of course I would! Thus was I convinced that God is concerned with us humans when we want Him enough. At long last I saw, I felt, I believed. Scales of pride and prejudice fell from my eyes. A new world came into view."[4]

Regarding the idea of "God" and finding God the NA book says this on page 25:

"In Narcotics Anonymous, we decide to turn our will and our lives over to the care of God as we understand Him. This is a giant step. We don't have to be religious; anyone can take this step. All that is required is willingness. All that is essential is that we open the door to a Power greater than ourselves."[5]

In many ways, the perspective regarding God and finding God, that is presented by both AA and NA, are very similar to what the Bible says as well. Jeremiah 29:12-14 says this about finding God:

"Then you will call on me and come and pray to me, and I will listen to you. [13] You will seek me and find me when you seek me with all your heart. [14] I will be found by you," declares the Lord, "and will bring you back from captivity." (NIV)

Wherever you are at with your thoughts about God, I encourage you to be open to God. I encourage you to seek to find God and I believe if you genuinely seek to find God, he will indeed reveal himself to you.

Just as Jesus said in John 14:6:

> "Jesus answered, "I am the way and the truth and the life. No one comes to the Father except through me."

The Twelve Steps of Recovery are very much about God and about a spiritual experience with God. A lot has been shared thus far in this chapter, but I think it might also be helpful to better understand how AA and NA integrate God into The Twelve Steps by simply reading The Twelve Steps of Recovery. So, here below are The Twelve Steps as given by Narcotics Anonymous:[6]

> 1. We admitted that we were powerless over our addiction, that our lives had become unmanageable.
>
> 2. We came to believe that a Power greater than ourselves could restore us to sanity.
>
> 3. We made a decision to turn our will and our lives over to the care of God as we understood Him.
>
> 4. We made a searching and fearless moral inventory of ourselves.
>
> 5. We admitted to God, to ourselves, and to another human being the exact nature of our wrongs.
>
> 6. We were entirely ready to have God remove all these defects of character.

7. We humbly asked Him to remove our shortcomings.

8 .We made a list of all persons we had harmed, and became willing to make amends to them all.

9. We made direct amends to such people wherever possible, except when to do so would injure them or others.

10. We continued to take personal inventory and when we were wrong promptly admitted it.

11. We sought through prayer and meditation to improve our conscious contact with God as we understood Him, praying only for knowledge of His will for us and the power to carry that out.

12. Having had a spiritual awakening as a result of these steps, we tried to carry this message to addicts, and to practice these principles in all our affairs.

The Twelve Steps of Recovery of AA and NA have indeed helped many millions of people to be successful in recovery. It is a program that has been proven by many people living full and abundant lives of recovery, free from the bondage of alcohol or drugs. The Twelve Steps of Recovery actually do work and finding God and having a spiritual experience with God is a central component of this program of recovery.

I encourage you to consider The Twelve Steps of Recovery for yourself and to also consider bringing God into your life and to begin a brand-new journey of recovery and even a brand-new life with God.

Step One:
We Admitted We Were Powerless

"We admitted that we were powerless
over our addiction, that our lives
had become unmanageable."[7]
(Step One from NA)

==================================

"And I know that nothing good lives in me,
that is, in my sinful nature. I want to do
what is right, but I can't."
(Romans 7:18 NLT)

==================================

"With Step One you have taken the most
important step. Now continue in your recovery
journey and do everything necessary to be
successful for recovery."[8]
(The Hope Recovery Devotional)

==================================

With this chapter we start at the beginning of The Twelve Steps of Recovery with Step One. The title of this chapter then is simply "Step One: We Admitted We Were Powerless".

The Twelve Steps of Recovery are very much about God and about having a spiritual experience with God, but Step One starts with admitting that we are powerless over our addiction. Step One as given by Narcotics Anonymous states:

> "We admitted that we were powerless over our addiction, that our lives had become unmanageable.[9]"

In the introduction to Step One in the book of Narcotics Anonymous it expresses the critical importance of Step One when it says this on page 20:

> "We are powerless not only over drugs, but over our addiction as well. We need to admit this fact in order to recover. Addiction is a physical, mental and spiritual disease that affects every area of our lives."[10]

In the book of Alcoholics Anonymous in the chapter called "How It Works" it describes the terrible power of alcohol and addiction when it states on page 58:

> "Remember that we deal with alcohol—cunning, baffling, powerful! Without help it is too much for

us. But there is One who has all power—that One is God."[11]

In these opening comments by the books of NA and AA it is clear how powerful alcohol and drugs are and that "we are powerless over our addiction" and "without help it is too much for us", but fortunately "there is One who has all power—that One is God." It is so important for Step One to start where it does, and it is also significant that both NA and AA indicate the spiritual component of recovery as well.

In my view there are four key principles of Step One, and many are foundational to building upon with the other steps.

You Are Not Alone
"WE admitted"

The first principle of Step One is that you do not need to go through recovery alone. Most of The Twelve Steps, as given by NA, start with the word "WE" and starting with "We" indicates that you do not need to go through recovery by yourself. While you might have been alone in your addiction you do not have to go through your recovery alone. You have many resources for support in the AA and NA fellowships, many faith-based recovery groups, and hopefully a church family and other family and friends that support your recovery. It is important that you intentionally seek to build your recovery community and to surround yourself with others that share your desire to be clean and sober and that share your love for God as well.

Admitting Our Condition
"We admitted we were powerless"

The second principle of Step One is all about admitting you are powerless. This is indeed a dramatic and humbling admission, but it is a critical admission for you to make and it is important that you do not attempt to explain it away. It is important for you to admit that this is where you are right now. Do not rationalize it away. It is not pleasant to admit this, but it is where you start with honestly admitting that in your own ability and willpower you are powerless.

In many ways Step One is really the most important step because it is with Step One all the others build upon. It is important to start at the beginning and to not skip over Step One. Step One will show if you are really committed to recovery. It is with Step One where you have the opportunity to start with rigorous honesty with yourself and others as you begin the journey of doing everything necessary to be successful in recovery.

Powerless Over Addiction
"We were powerless over our addiction"

The next principle is that you identify and declare exactly what you are powerless over and that is your addiction. It is one thing to admit that you have a problem, or you have trouble with something, but it is quite another to admit that you are powerless over your addiction! This is a great admission and shows that you are being completely and brutally honest with your lack of power. NA speaks to this condition of being powerless over addiction when they state on page 21:

> "Most of us tried to stop using on our own, but we were unable to live with or without drugs. Eventually we realized that we were powerless over our addiction."[12]

It is important to be brutally honest and to admit your powerless condition over your addiction as this is a foundational step for success in recovery. To be successful in recovery, you need to first recognize your addiction.

Honestly Look at Our Lives
"Our lives had become unmanageable"

The fourth and last principle of Step One is to honestly look at the condition of your life and then to admit the truth about your life that has become unmanageable. It is important to admit you are powerless over your addiction and it is also important to admit your life has become unmanageable. I encourage you to resist the impulse to minimize the damage to your life and to minimize the circumstances of your life, as this is again an important time to be brutally honest with yourself.

As you admit your life has become unmanageable, you may also feel that you have failed in every way. You may feel that there is nothing good about you and the things you have done in your addiction. The Bible passage for today is from Romans 7:18 may reflect how you feel about yourself right now which says:

> "And I know that nothing good lives in me, that is, in my sinful nature. I want to do what is right, but I can't." (Romans 7:18 NLT)

This verse is also very much like the quote from page 25 of the AA *Big Book* that simply says:

> "So many want to stop but cannot."[13]

This passage in Romans and this quote from AA may describe the way you feel about yourself right now. You may feel there is nothing good in you and that while you want to stop, you can't. This passage describes the condition of the addict. So many want to stop but cannot. You may feel hopeless. But the first step to recovery and to a right relationship with God is to admit you are powerless over your addiction and ultimately to admit you are powerless over sin. This passage from Romans absolutely describes the condition of the addict saying, "I want to do what is right, but I can't." Perhaps these are words you have said many times. But I want you to understand that this passage is evidence that God knows you and understands you and that God does indeed want to help you be successful in recovery and to not stay in your addiction. A few verses later in Romans

7:24-25 God declares he has provided a solution for our condition:

> "What a wretched man I am! Who will rescue me from this body that is subject to death? [25] Thanks be to God, who delivers me through Jesus Christ our Lord!" (Romans 7:24-25 NIV)

With Step One you have taken the most important step. Now continue in your recovery journey of The Twelve Steps of Recovery with the singular focus to do everything necessary to be successful in recovery. Yes, recovery is absolutely possible, and it all starts with Step One of Recovery.

Brief Summary of Step One

"We admitted that we were powerless over our addiction, that our lives had become unmanageable."[14]
(Step One from NA)

1) You are Not Alone
  a. "WE admitted."
2) Admitting Our Condition
  a. "We admitted we were powerless."
3) Powerless Over Addiction
  a. "We were powerless over our addiction."
4) Honestly Look at Our Lives
  a. "Our lives had become unmanageable."

Step One
Additional Bible Passages

Romans 7:18 (NLT)
And I know that nothing good lives in me, that is, in my sinful nature. I want to do what is right, but I can't.

Genesis 3:1-2 (NKJV)
Now the serpent was more cunning than any beast of the field which the Lord God had made. And he said to the woman, "Has God indeed said, 'You shall not eat of every tree of the garden'?"

Jeremiah 17:9 (NKJV)
The heart *is* deceitful above all *things,* And desperately wicked; Who can know it?

Romans 3:22-24 (NKJV)
For there is no difference; [23] for all have sinned and fall short of the glory of God, [24] being justified freely by His grace through the redemption that is in Christ Jesus.

2 Peter 3:9 (ESV)
The Lord is not slow to fulfill his promise as some count slowness, but is patient toward you, not wishing that any should perish, but that all should reach repentance.

Romans 5:8 (NKJV)
But God demonstrates His own love toward us, in that while we were still sinners, Christ died for us.

Step Two:
A Power Greater Than Ourselves

"We came to believe that a Power greater than ourselves could restore us to sanity."[15]
(Step Two from NA)

==================================

"For God is working in you, giving you the desire and the power to do what pleases him."
(Philippians 2:13 NLT)

==================================

"Allow yourself to believe there is a power greater than yourself that can help you to be restored to sanity."[16]
(The Hope Recovery Devotional)

==================================

The title of this chapter is simply "Step Two: A Power Greater Than Ourselves". Step Two of Recovery as given by NA states:

> "We came to believe that a Power greater than ourselves could restore us to sanity."[17]

Step Two is all about power, but specifically about "a Power greater than ourselves" and this Step Two follows on from Step One which also talks about power. But in Step One "We admitted that we were powerless over our addiction, that our lives had become unmanageable.[18]" So briefly, in Step One we admitted "we were powerless over our addiction" and this is indeed a tremendous admission to acknowledge that we are "powerless" over our addiction. For anyone in addiction this is a great truth to acknowledge and to embrace as being true for you, that you are powerless over your addiction. But Step Two does not leave you there as being powerless. Step Two talks about "A Power greater than ourselves" because in our own power and in our own strength we did not have the power to overcome our addiction.

The AA book on page 45 from the chapter "We Agnostics" talks about this idea of power of both Step One and Step Two when it states:

> "Our human resources, as marshalled by the will, were not sufficient; they failed utterly. Lack of power, that was our dilemma. We had to find a power by which we could live, and it had to be a *Power greater than ourselves.* Obviously. But

where and how were we to find this Power? Well, that's exactly what this book is about. Its main object is to enable you to find a Power greater than yourself which will solve your problem."[19]

There is much to be taken from Step Two, but in my view there are three main principles, including that Step Two takes many important steps "of beginning". And in many ways Step Two is the beginning of faith and hope as well.

The Beginning of Faith
"We came to believe"

The first principle is the beginning of faith as is reflected in the quote of "We came to believe". In many ways Step Two is the beginning of faith. It is yet a very small expression of faith. But in some small way Step Two begins the process of "believing". It is not important to fully understand who this "higher power" is just yet, but it is important to have faith to believe that there is somewhere, somehow a "Power" greater than ourselves.

Through the Twelve Steps of Recovery many millions of people over many decades of time have been successful in recovery. So, even if you simply start with the faith of believing that these millions of people, that have been successful in recovery, are the evidence there is a "power greater than yourself" that is a fine place to start. The beginning of faith can be to believe in the power that worked for so many others to be successful in recovery and that same power can work for you as well.

The Beginning of Accepting a Higher Power
"A Power greater than ourselves"

Principle two is the beginning of accepting a higher power as "A Power greater than ourselves". Step Two is also the beginning of accepting help from a "higher power". You are not there just yet, but you are now convinced you need help beyond yourself. You are thoroughly convinced that you do not have the necessary power yourself to be successful in recovery. If you did, you would have been clean and sober a long time ago. But you do believe there is a "power greater" than yourself that can help you in your recovery.

It is ok that right now you are not entirely clear on exactly what this power or this "higher power" looks like or who he is. But you know it is only with a higher power, a "power greater" than yourself, that you can be successful in recovery. So, you believe that with a "power greater" than yourself, you can be successful in recovery and this enables you to continue on.

The Beginning of a Return to Sanity
"Could Restore Us to Sanity"

Principle three is the beginning of a return to sanity with the expression that this higher power "could restore us to sanity." Step One says that your life "had become unmanageable" which is another way of saying your life was in chaos, your life was falling apart. But it is with Step Two that gives you the hope this "higher power" could "restore you to sanity"; that this "higher power" could restore your life to sanity. It likely would not be overnight, but this "higher power" would give you the power to begin to bring sanity into your life. It won't be fast, and it will likely be painful, but with this "power greater than yourself" it is possible. Recovery is now possible.

This leads me to the Bible passage for Step Two from Philippians 4:13 (ESV) that says:

> "I can do all things through him who strengthens me."

Your recovery might seem impossible to you right now. You may have tried recovery or rehab many, many times and yet you were still not able to be successful in recovery. But this Bible verse from Philippians 4:13 seems to speak to this very topic saying, "I can do all things", even recover from years of alcohol or drug addiction, "through him who strengthens me." Consider this passage as you go further in Step Two and even later as you look at the rest of The Twelve Steps of Recovery and remember the passage "I can do all things through him who strengthens me." Recovery is absolutely possible with a "power greater than yourself" with the true "higher power".

It is with this coming "to believe" in a "Power greater" than yourself that your life could be "restored to sanity." That is indeed faith and hope and not hope in yourself or even any other person, but faith and hope in a "higher power" in a "Power greater" than yourself. That is how you can have true hope when you put your hope in God the true "higher power".

The wording of Step Two is very much an expression of faith. Step Two of Recovery says, "We came to believe that a Power greater than ourselves could restore us to sanity.[20]" That is the beginning of faith and of hope as well.

I encourage you to embrace this idea of faith and wherever you are at in your faith and with your belief in a "higher power" and with God I encourage you to continue to seek to find God and I believe if you genuinely seek to find God you will indeed find him and you will find that this true "higher power" does indeed have the power to restore your life to sanity and the power to help you to be successful in recovery and even to a brand new life as well.

Brief Summary of Step Two

"We came to believe that a Power greater than ourselves
could restore us to sanity."[21]
(Step Two from NA)

1) The Beginning of Faith
    a. "We came to believe".
2) The Beginning of Accepting a "Higher Power"
    a. "A Power greater than ourselves."
3) The Beginning of a Return to Sanity
    a. "Could restore us to sanity."

Step Two
Additional Bible Passages

Philippians 2:13 (NLT)
For God is working in you, giving you the desire and the power to do what pleases him.

Proverbs 12:20 (ESV)
Deceit is in the heart of those who devise evil, but those who plan peace have joy.

Mark 9:24 (NKJV)
Immediately the father of the child cried out and said with tears, "Lord, I believe; help my unbelief!"

Matthew 8:26 (ESV)
And he said to them, "Why are you afraid, O you of little faith?" Then he rose and rebuked the winds and the sea, and there was a great calm.

James 1:5 (ESV)
If any of you lacks wisdom, let him ask God, who gives generously to all without reproach, and it will be given him.

John 16:33 (NIV)
I have told you these things, so that in me you may have peace. In this world you will have trouble. But take heart! I have overcome the world.

"We made a decision to turn our will
and our lives over to the care of God
as we understood him."[22]
(Step Three from NA)

==

"For it is by grace you have been saved,
through faith and this is not from yourselves,
it is the gift of God."
(Ephesians 2:8 NIV)

==

"This decision is another way of making an
expression of faith that you can trust God."[23]
(The Hope Recovery Devotional)

==

Step Three of Recovery is a pretty dramatic step as it is all about making a life-changing decision. Step Three of Recovery, as given by Narcotics Anonymous states:

> "We made a decision to turn our will and our lives over to the care of God as we understood Him."[24]

This Step is ultimately all about making a decision, but more specifically making a decision for God. And so, the title of this chapter is simply "Step Three: Made a Decision for God".

The first Three Steps of Recovery are often paraphrased simply as "I can't, God can, I think I'll let him". So briefly, in Step One we admitted 'we were powerless over our addiction', in Step Two 'we came to believe there was a power greater than ourselves', and in Step Three 'we made a decision for God'. We made a decision for this "greater power" or for this "higher power".

The Alcoholics Anonymous *Big Book* on page 62 from the chapter "How it Works" says this about Step Three:

> "First of all, we had to quit playing God. It didn't work. Next, we decided that hereafter in this drama of life, God was going to be our Director. He is the Principal; we are His agents. He is the Father, and we are His children. Most good ideas are simple, and this concept was the keystone of the new and triumphant arch through which we passed to freedom."[25]

This quote from AA says that "Most good ideas are simple" and so I encourage you to not over-complicate this step. Keep it simple. Step Three is all about making a decision for God. And the Narcotics Anonymous book continues this message and goes even deeper when it says this on page 25, also from the NA chapter "How it Works":

> "For all of us, the day came when there was no longer a choice; we had to use. Having given our will and lives to our addiction, in utter desperation, we looked for another way. In Narcotics Anonymous, we decide to turn our will and our lives over to the care of God as we understand Him. This is a giant step. We don't have to be religious; anyone can take this step. All that is required is willingness. All that is essential is that we open the door to a Power greater than ourselves."[26]

This quote from NA also indicates that while this is "a giant step" it is also a simple step stating simply "All that is required is willingness" and so I again encourage you to not over-complicate this step. You "do not have to be religious; anyone can take this step."

As I look at Step Three of Recovery, and this life-changing decision, there are in my view four key principles.

You Are Not Alone
"WE made a decision"

First is this perspective, that you are not alone with the quote "We made a decision". The Twelve Steps of Recovery as given by NA start with "We". And this indicates that you do not go through recovery alone. Recovery is meant to be done in a recovery community. This is an important principle that you are not alone. While you may have been alone in your addiction, you are not alone in your recovery! And now with Step Three and your decision for God, God is with you as well. Community will include your recovery community of AA or NA fellowships, but also your faith-based recovery groups, perhaps with Celebrate Recovery and other faith-based recovery groups. And, eventually a supportive and welcoming church fellowship as well.

Making a Decision for God
"We made a decision"

The next principle is all about making a decision for God with some expression of faith as reflected with the quote "We Made a Decision". In Step Three you make a conscious decision for God. This means you have made a decision to trust God. By trusting God, you acknowledge God does indeed exist, and that God is a loving, caring, and compassionate God, who absolutely wants to help you. This decision may be by saying a simple prayer or by crying out to God, but it is a conscious and intentional decision for God, and an intentional decision to trust God as well.

Turning Your Life Over to God
"Turn our will and lives over to the care of God"

Principle three reflects making a dramatic life-changing decision. Step Three is a pretty dramatic step as you make the decision of turning your life over to God, as expressed with the words "turn our will and our lives over to the care of God". The conscious decision that you make is to turn your life over to God and this means turning your will over to God such that now you want to seek God's will for your life and then to live that out in your life each day and one day at a time. Your goal is not to seek your own will, which was what you have done in the past, but to now actually seek to know and to follow God's will in your life. This principle also means that you start to simply trust God. To trust that God knows what is best for you and that you can trust God to care for you and to trust that God knows what is best for you and ultimately that God will help you to be successful in recovery.

Start at the Beginning of Faith
"As we understood Him"

Principle four acknowledges that you start right where you are; you start at the beginning of faith wherever that might be for you as the quote indicates "as we understood Him". Making a decision for God is a decision of faith in God, it is an expression of faith in God that you now are just beginning to put your trust in

God for all aspects of your life. Step Three means to start wherever you are at in your belief in God with whatever your understanding is of God. It is all ok. But you start with an expression of faith in God. You start at the beginning wherever you are at with God. It does not mean you have God all figured out and that you know all the answers about God, but it does mean that you are making the decision to seek to know God more and more each day and to seek his will in your life. And that you are turning your will and life over to God, however he may direct you in your recovery and in your life as well.

Step Three of Recovery can be a very freeing step. You now are letting God direct your life. Now you are not in control, but you are making the decision to turn your will and life over to God and that you can trust God with your life and that now God will be in control. Step Three can be the very beginning of your freedom from addiction and the beginning of a brand-new life as well.

Step Three of Recovery is a great step and I believe the Bible passage of Proverbs 3:5-6 relates well to this Step and the decision for God and to trust God. Proverbs 3:5-6 says:

> "Trust in the Lord with all your heart and lean not on your own understanding; [6] in all your ways submit to him, and he will make your paths straight."

33

Step Three is a very important step. It is a foundational step for your recovery. Recovery is absolutely possible, and it all begins by making a decision for God, with making a conscious and intentional decision for God and turning your will and life over to the care of God. You can trust God to guide and direct your life and your recovery. As you trust God with "all your heart" and "lean not on your own understanding" I encourage you to "submit to him" and he will direct your paths. With Step Three of Recovery begin at the beginning of faith and seek each day to grow in knowledge of God and to know his will in your life. Recovery is absolutely possible, and it all begins with making a decision for God.

I encourage you to consider making a decision for God yourself and making a personal decision for God, to trust God and to turn your will and life over to the care of God. God is a loving, caring, and compassionate God who wants to help you. God wants to help you to be successful in recovery and even in a brand-new life with him.

Brief Summary of Step Three

"We made a decision to turn our will and our lives over to the care of God as we understood him."[27]
(Step Three from NA)

1) You are Not Alone
    a. "WE made a decision."
2) Making a Decision for God
    a. "We Made a Decision."
3) Turning Your Life Over to God
    a. "Turn our will and our lives over to the care of God".
4) Start at the Beginning of Faith
    a. "As we understood Him."

Step Three:
Additional Bible Passages

Ephesians 2:8 (NIV)
For it is by grace you have been saved, through faith and this is not from yourselves, it is the gift of God.

Deuteronomy 31:6 (NIV)
Be strong and courageous. Do not be afraid or terrified because of them, for the Lord your God goes with you; he will never leave you nor forsake you.

Proverbs 3:5-6 (NJKV)
Trust in the Lord with all your heart, And lean not on your own understanding; [6] In all your ways acknowledge Him, And He shall direct your paths.

Psalm 56:3 (NIV)
When I am afraid, I put my trust in you.

John 14:1 (ESV)
Let not your hearts be troubled. Believe in God; believe also in me.

John 3:16 (NIV)
For God so loved the world that he gave his one and only Son, that whoever believes in him shall not perish but have eternal life.

Step Four:
Made a Fearless Moral Inventory

"We made a searching and fearless moral
inventory of ourselves."[28]
(Step Four from NA)

==

"Search me, God, and know my heart;
test me and know my anxious thoughts.
[24]See if there is any offensive way in me,
and lead me in the way everlasting."
(Psalm 139:23-24 NIV)

==

"Please understand, regardless of the negative
aspects of your past and of your moral
inventory, that does not change the fact
God loves you."[29]
(The Hope Recovery Devotional)

==

This chapter is on Step Four of Recovery. Step Four begins a different direction than the first three steps. The first three steps are the beginning of restoring our relationship with God, but in the next several steps we begin to look more closely at ourselves. The *Big Book* of AA ends the discussion of Step Three and this idea of making a decision for God when it states this on page 63:

> "This was only a beginning, though if honestly and humbly made, an effect, sometimes a very great one, was felt at once."[30]

Step Three and making a decision for God for your higher power was indeed a very important step and often a very dramatic step as well. But, the first three steps simply lay the groundwork, the foundation for growing in our spiritual life and our spiritual experience with God. Step Four begins the process of taking a "moral inventory". Before we go any further here is Step Four as given by Narcotics Anonymous:

> "We made a searching and fearless moral inventory of ourselves."[31]

But what does this really mean? What is a "moral inventory"? Let me give you a couple of quotes from AA and NA that might help clarify what is intended by this Step Four. It is helpful to hear how the *Big Book* of AA introduces Step Four on page 64 when it states:

"Therefore, we started upon a personal inventory. *This was Step Four.* A business which takes no regular inventory usually goes broke. Taking a commercial inventory is a fact-finding and a fact-facing process. It is an effort to discover the truth about the stock-in trade. One object is to disclose damaged or unsalable goods, to get rid of them promptly and without regret. If the owner of the business is to be successful, he cannot fool himself about values."[32]

AA compares the personal inventory of Step Four to taking a "commercial inventory" in essence to find the character traits that for us are "damaged or unsalable goods" and then AA says to "get rid of them promptly and without regret." The book of NA also gives guidance on Step Four that is quite similar to AA when it states on page 30:

"The important thing is to write a moral inventory. If the word moral bothers us, we may call it a positive/negative inventory."[33]

Many have found that Step Four is very difficult, and it makes people quite fearful to even consider honestly and thoroughly doing Step Four and making a personal moral inventory of all the bad from the past. But the book of NA helps to prepare us for doing Step Four and NA speaks about how to overcome this fear, so that we can do Step Four honestly. Regarding this fear of the past NA says on page 27:

"We have found that fear is a lack of faith, and we have found a loving, personal God to whom we can turn. We no longer need to be afraid."[34]

With our newfound relationship with God, as our higher power, he will help us to be honest and fearless in taking our moral inventory. And NA emphasizes this point of God's help when it states on page 29:

"Writing a thorough and honest inventory seemed impossible. It was, as long as we were operating under our own power. We take a few quiet moments before writing and ask for the strength to be fearless and thorough."[35]

With that quote from NA we are reminded to ask God for help, and he will indeed give us the strength to be fearless in Step Four.

Let me suggest that there are 4 main principles for Step Four of Recovery and, as with the other Steps as given by NA Step Four also starts with "We" and so it highlights that you are not alone, as do all the Steps as given by NA. While this is not the main point here it is a consistent theme and reminder that The Twelve Steps, beginning with "We", highlights the importance of being part of a recovery community.

Just Make a List
"We made a moral inventory"

The first principle is to just make a list, as in "We made a moral inventory" list. The main thought of this first key principle is that you are going to make a list. You are not yet taking any action with the list or with anyone else, you are simply making a list. And it is recommended that you actually write the list out, that you write it or type it or put it in your phone. It is not enough to think about it or to talk about it. You need to write it out in a list and enter it somewhere. Do not get bogged down with any other thoughts or emotions wherever these positive or negative entries may take you, but here you are just making the list. And so, the first key principle of Step Four is to just make a list.

Be Fearless
"We made a searching and fearless moral inventory"

The next key principle is to be fearless, as in "We made a searching and fearless moral inventory". Step Four is not a casual or light-hearted search, but it is a searching and fearless investigation into your moral inventory. Being fearless in your searching indicates it is a brutally honest searching process. You do not leave anything hidden, but you expose it and then add it to your list. In my view, NA takes a broader perspective of Step Four and is more open to considering the bad and the good character traits. So, I would suggest anything that your fearless searching has uncovered, whether bad or even good, is added to the list. It is only when you make this searching and fearless list that you can know what to discard and what to keep, removing the bad and building upon the good.

Take the Moral Inventory
"We made a moral inventory"

The third principle is to actually take the moral inventory as in "We made a moral inventory". The actual taking of the moral inventory can be difficult. Perhaps, as a starting place for the negative inventory consider such character traits as resentment, guilt, dishonesty, selfishness, and anger, and others as your searching reveals. And then perhaps consider more specific instances of each. Likewise, for the positive inventory consider gratitude, sharing, courage, and even your new faith and many others here too and then to also consider specific instances of each for your list. Be bold and fearless in your search as you look at both your bad and good moral inventory and write it all down on your list.

Make it Personal
"A moral inventory of ourselves"

This next principle may be even more of a challenge as it requires you are to make it personal, as in "A moral inventory of ourselves". The whole point of Step Four is for you to make a searching and fearless moral inventory list of yourself! It is often much easier to see the character defects in others such as, your spouse, your friends, your co-workers, or anyone else. But this step is for you to make a searching and fearless moral inventory list of yourself! And that will indeed require you to do a searching and fearless investigation. This will indeed take courage to be brutally honest and that is what will make Step Four an important step for you and for your recovery. By being honest of both the positive and negative aspects of your moral inventory, that is part of the process that helps you to be successful in recovery. In addition, that is part of the process to help you live in this new world of a spiritual experience with God as well.

The NA book summarizes Step Four with a focus on what the goal of Step Four really is and so on page 30 NA says:

> "We sit down with paper and pen and ask for our God's help in revealing the defects that are causing pain and suffering. We pray for the courage to be fearless and thorough and that this inventory may help us to put our lives in order. When we pray and take action, it always goes better for us."[36]

Step Four of Recovery is an important step, and it will not be easy and it will indeed take courage. The Bible passage of Psalm 139:23-24 relates well to this Step Four of Recovery and how God can help you in this process. Psalm 139:23-24 says:

> "Search me, God, and know my heart; test me and know my anxious thoughts. [24] See if there is any

offensive way in me, and lead me in the way everlasting."

This Bible passage brings together many of the same principles of Step Four. Here the prayer of the writer and for you is asking God for help in the searching process to search your heart and thoughts and to reveal any offensive way. Then the prayer goes on saying to lead you in the way everlasting, or in other words to lead you in a life that honors God. Step Four is all about asking God to help you make this moral inventory list and to do it in a way that is searching and fearless so that God can guide you to know what to do with what you find. And through this process, God will help you to be successful in recovery and God will lead you to a brand-new life as well.

Brief Summary of Step Four

"We made a searching and fearless
moral inventory of ourselves."[37]
(Step Four from NA)

1) Just Make a List
    a. "We made a moral inventory".
2) Be Fearless
    a. "We made a searching and fearless moral inventory."
3) Take the Moral Inventory
    a. "We made a moral inventory".
4) Make it Personal
    a. "A moral inventory of ourselves".

Step Four:
Additional Bible Passages

Psalm 139:23-24 (NIV)
Search me, God, and know my heart; test me and know my anxious thoughts. [24]See if there is any offensive way in me, and lead me in the way everlasting.

Hebrews 4:12 (NIV)
For the word of God is alive and active. Sharper than any double-edged sword, it penetrates even to dividing soul and spirit, joints and marrow; it judges the thoughts and attitudes of the heart.

Romans 12:2 (ESV)
Do not be conformed to this world, but be transformed by the renewal of your mind, that by testing you may discern what is the will of God, what is good and acceptable and perfect.

Psalm 19:14 (ESV)
Let the words of my mouth and the meditation of my heart be acceptable in your sight, O Lord, my rock and my redeemer.

Proverbs 11:3 (ESV)
The integrity of the upright guides them, but the crookedness of the treacherous destroys them.

Step Five:
We Admitted to God Our Wrongs

"We admitted to God, to ourselves,
and to another human being,
the exact nature of our wrongs."[38]
(Step Five from NA)

===================================

"Then I acknowledged my sin to you
and did not cover up my iniquity. I said,
'I will confess my transgressions to the Lord.'
And you forgave the guilt of my sin."
(Psalm 32:5 NIV)

===================================

"Confessing to God is where our spiritual
healing starts, and then it continues with
confessing to ourselves... and accepting
responsibility for what we have done."[39]
(The Hope Recovery Devotional)

===================================

This chapter is on Step Five of Recovery. Step Five continues in this new direction that was started in Step Four. In Step Four we made a "Searching and fearless moral inventory of ourselves" and Step Five builds upon this "moral inventory" that we made in Step Four. Step Five as given in Narcotics Anonymous reads like this:

"We admitted to God, to ourselves, and to another human being the exact nature of our wrongs."[40]

So, Step Five is all based upon this fearless moral inventory of Step Four. In Step Four we made a searching and fearless moral inventory list of ourselves, but it is not enough to simply make the list of Step Four. And while Step Four and making the list is a very important step, Step Five takes it even further and then requires action on our part. Step Five requires action on the moral inventory list of Step Four. Alcoholics Anonymous speaks to this action when it states on page 72:

"This requires action on our part, which, when completed, will mean that we have admitted to God, to ourselves, and to another human being, the exact nature of our defects."[41]

NA speaks to this perspective when it states on page 31:

"After taking a thorough Fourth Step, we deal with the contents of our inventory. We are told that if we keep these defects inside us, they will lead us back to using. Holding on to our past would eventually sicken us and keep us from taking part in our new way of life (and later...) "It would be tragic to write it all down and then shove it in a drawer. These defects grow in the dark, and die in the light of exposure."[42]

Step Five will be difficult. It will be difficult to admit our defects to God and it will be especially difficult to share our defects with another human being. But I encourage you to remember that while it will be difficult, it is a step that will lead to freedom. Step Five is an action step that NA says on page 31:

> "The Fifth Step is the key to freedom. It allows us to live clean in the present. Sharing the exact nature of our wrongs sets us free to live. After taking a thorough Fourth Step, we deal with the contents of our inventory."[43]

Step Five is an action step, and it is a hard step to perform, but AA and NA both indicate that God will indeed help you through this step. In fact, both AA and NA indicate that Step Five is a dramatic step forward in your spiritual life and your spiritual connection with God. AA states it this way on page 75:

> "We may have had certain spiritual beliefs, but now we begin to have a spiritual experience (... and later) We thank God from the bottom of our heart that we know Him better."[44]

Step Five is a big step forward in our spiritual life and in our relationship with God and even though it will be difficult God will indeed help us carry out this step. So, again Step Five from NA reads as:

"We admitted to God, to ourselves, and to another human being the exact nature of our wrongs."[45]

Let me suggest that there are 5 main principles for Step Five of Recovery. And as with the other Steps, as given by NA, Step Five also starts with "WE" and so it highlights that you are not alone, you are not alone in your recovery.

We Admitted
"We confessed our sins and failures"

In Step Five we admitted, as in "We confessed our sins and failures". The main point with this first principle is one of confession that you honestly admitted and confessed and acknowledged your sins and your failures. This is the time to be brutally honest with yourself. Hiding any secrets now will only come back to pull you down at some point in the future. Take advantage of this opportunity to finally be honest with yourself. It is with being completely honest with Step Five, and all of The Twelve Steps that will give you a new sense of freedom and liberty from the past and even that will take your spiritual relationship with God even further.

Admitted to God
"We confessed our sins and failures to God"

Here we simply admitted to God, as in "We confessed our sins and failures to God". You may feel why is this needed doesn't God already know. And indeed, God does know, but it is important for you to know it as well. It is important for you to express it to God in admitting it to God and in confessing it to God. To not admit it to God now would be a way of rationalizing this important principle away. It is important for this admission and confession to come from your own voice and in your own words of confession to God. God will honor this act of obedience and it will be an important part of nurturing your spiritual relationship with God.

Admitted to Ourselves
"We took responsibility"

The next principle of Step Five is we admitted to ourselves, as in "We took responsibility". This is the time to view ourselves in a realistic way. In the past you might have changed your view of things to appear more favorable for you so you might not look so bad. But now is the time to look at yourself honestly and in a realistic manner. It is time to take responsibility for your actions. Do not leave your past failures in the dark to remain hidden but bring them fully out in the light. God is a compassionate God, and he will help you through this process and he will guide you so that this will be a very liberating experience and one that you can indeed grow in your faith and grow in your sense of freedom from the past.

Admitted to Another Human Being
"We confessed to another trusted individual"

In this principle we admitted to another human being, as in "We confessed to another trusted individual". Unlike the other previous steps this step requires that you work with someone else. You need to talk with another person to complete this step and you need to admit some very difficult sins and failures to another human being. This will indeed be difficult, but of course most of the really valuable things in life are not easy and this is no exception. As human beings, we do not like to share deeply personal thoughts with others, and that is why it is critical that you select an individual that you can trust completely, someone that will understand the magnitude of this process and that really understands that these Twelve Steps of Recovery are really a matter of life or death. So, choose this person wisely and make sure they completely understand what you are doing and how it is a critical part of The Twelve Steps of Recovery. And then sit down and get ready for a long conversation with this trusted individual. Certainly, men should share with men and women should share with women.

Admitted the Exact Nature of Our Wrongs
"We were specific with our failures"

Here the point is to be specific. We admitted the exact nature of our wrongs, as in "We were specific with our failures". This is a significant part of Step Five. We are to be specific. We are to be exact. This is not the time to generalize, but to recall specific instances of our failures and they are what we are to admit and to confess. It is with this aspect of being specific or being exact that will help us recognize patterns of our past behavior that need correcting. While it is not possible to recall each and every past failure, it is important to give this our best effort to remember as much as possible. This will help with admitting, with confessing, and correcting later on as well.

The whole point of Step Five is for you to admit your wrongs first to God, then to yourself, and then to another human being. This Step Five process is a process that can lead to freedom. Freedom from the past, but also it can be a tremendous time of growth, spiritual growth and growth in your relationship with God. NA on page 33 speaks to this when it states:

> "We begin to experience real personal feelings of a spiritual nature. Where once we had spiritual theories, we now begin to awaken to spiritual reality."[46]

Step Five of Recovery is an important and difficult step, but with God's help it can be a wonderful opportunity to confess your past sins and failures and to expose them with the light of God's truth. Regardless of what you have done in the past and regardless of what you admitted to and confessed to; I encourage you to remember that God will absolutely forgive you. And God will use this process of confession as a way for you to grow in your relationship with God. It can truly be a time for these spiritual beliefs to become a true spiritual experience with God as you confess your sins and your failures to God and then as you sense God's amazing forgiveness as well.

Step Five is all about admitting and confessing our sins and failures to God and with this as the focus I believe the passage from Psalm 32:5 relates well to Step Five when it states:

> "Then I acknowledged my sin to you and did not cover up my iniquity. I said, "I will confess my transgressions to the Lord. And you forgave the guilt of my sin."

Step Five of Recovery can be a dramatic step in your recovery by honestly admitting your past failures and confessing them to God and to another human being. And as this passage from Psalm 32:5 tells us God is not a harsh or mean-spirited God and he does not want to punish us for our past sins, but rather the heart of God is one of forgiveness. God does indeed want to forgive us and to forgive you. As you go through Step Five and even life in general, please remember, that God does indeed want to forgive you and that the God of the Bible is a loving, caring, compassionate, and forgiving God and he does indeed want to help you. You may feel your past sins are terrible and you may wonder if God will even forgive you for these terrible sins, please know that he will. While you may have trouble accepting God's forgiveness, I encourage you to remember the truth of the Bible and of Psalm 32:5 that says:

> "Then I acknowledged my sin to you and did not cover up my iniquity. I said, "I will confess my transgressions to the Lord. And you forgave the guilt of my sin."

Yes, God will indeed forgive you whenever you admit your sins and confess them to him.

Brief Summary of Step Five

"We admitted to God, to ourselves, and to another human being, the exact nature of our wrongs."[47]
(Step Five from NA)

1) We Admitted
   a. "We confessed our sins and failures".
2) Admitted to God
   a. "We confessed our sins and failures to God".
3) Admitted to Ourselves
   a. "We took responsibility".
4) Admitted to Another Human Being
   a. "We confessed to another trusted individual".
5) Admitted the Exact Nature of Our Wrongs
   a. "We were specific with our failures".

Step Five:
Additional Bible Passages

Psalm 32:5 (NIV)
Then I acknowledged my sin to you and did not cover up my iniquity. I said, "I will confess my transgressions to the Lord." And you forgave the guilt of my sin.

Proverbs 28:13 (NKJV)
He who covers his sins will not prosper, But whoever confesses and forsakes *them* will have mercy.

James 5:15 (NIV)
Therefore confess your sins to each other and pray for each other so that you may be healed. The prayer of a righteous person is powerful and effective.

Psalm 103:10-12 (NKJV)
He has not dealt with us according to our sins, Nor punished us according to our iniquities. [11] For as the heavens are high above the earth, *So* great is His mercy toward those who fear Him; [12] As far as the east is from the west, *So* far has He removed our transgressions from us.

1 John 2:1 (NIV)
My dear children, I write this to you so that you will not sin. But if anybody does sin, we have an advocate with the Father—Jesus Christ, the Righteous One.

Step Six:
Ready for God to Remove Our Defects

"We were entirely ready to have God remove all
these defects of character."[48]
(Step Six from NA)

==================================

"I will give them a new heart and a new mind.
I will take away their stubborn heart of stone
and will give them an obedient heart."
(Ezekiel 11:19 GNT)

==================================

"Our part is to be ready and willing for God to
remove all our character defects."[49]
(The Hope Recovery Devotional)

==================================

This chapter of Step Six of Recovery continues the direction of Step Four and Step Five with our moral inventory and then admitting to God the exact nature of our wrongs. But, in Step Six we are directed to consider if we are really ready. Are we really ready for the dramatic change that The Twelve Steps of Recovery demand? Step Six as given in Narcotics Anonymous reads:

"We were entirely ready to have God remove all these defects of character."[50]

On the surface this seems to be a rather straightforward Step and even a very reasonable Step. When we unpack it further and really consider what this Step is asking of us, then we begin to understand the dramatic change that this Step is asking us to make. Narcotics Anonymous introduces this topic of Step Six with this perspective on page 34 when it states:

"Why ask for something before we are ready for it? This would be asking for trouble. So many times addicts have sought the rewards of hard work without the labor. Willingness is what we strive for in Step Six. How sincerely we work this step will be proportionate to our desire for change."[51]

And then later NA goes further and states:

"We pray or otherwise become willing, ready and able to let God remove these destructive traits. We need a personality change, if we are to stay clean. We want to change."[52]

These two quotes from NA speak a lot about "change", about a "personality change" and about a "willingness" to make this change. This "personality change" indicates a deep fundamental change within ourselves and in order to make this fundamental change we absolutely need to be "willing" and so "willingness" is needed for Step Six. So again, Step Six from NA is given as:

"We were entirely ready to have God remove all these defects of character."[53]

Let me suggest that there are three main principles for Step Six of Recovery and as with the other Steps as given by NA Step Six also starts with "We" to emphasize that in recovery you are not alone. You work out your recovery within a recovery community.

Were Entirely Ready
"We were ready and willing for change"

Are you really ready? Here in this step, we came to the point where we were entirely ready, as in "We were ready and willing for change". From the moral inventory list of Step Four we are now ready, entirely ready, to begin this process that leads to a dramatic change in our character. As NA indicated it is important to be ready for this change or "Why ask for something before we are ready for it?" It is also important to understand that the quote is "entirely ready", which indicates a thorough and complete process leaving nothing behind and nothing beyond evaluation. But it does not mean that it will be quick or fast. In fact, it will be a life-long process of yielding to God as he removes our defects of character. It is also important to not feel overwhelmed with thinking how can you address all these defects of character all at once. Prayerfully seek God's direction and he will show you which "defects" he wants you to work on first. God will show you his priority, likely the first priorities are the ones that might put you most at risk of picking up a drink or a drug again or stated another way the "defects" that might put you most at risk of a relapse.

Have God Remove
"God will remove the defects not us"

It is not all up to us. Here we need to be ready to have God remove, as in "God will remove the defects not us". NA states quite clearly that we are not doing the work we are not doing the removing, but it is God who is doing the work. NA says that we need to "become willing, ready and able to let God remove these destructive traits". This point is brought out in the book by Dale and Juanita Ryan called *The Twelve Steps: A Spiritual Kindergarten* where they state:

> "It is time to prepare for God to do spiritual and psychological surgery on our character."[54]

You need to be entirely ready and willing and then God will do the spiritual and psychological surgery to remove your defects of character. With this perspective you are the ready and willing patient ready for surgery and God is the surgeon. You need to let God be God and let him do his surgery removing your character defects.

Remove All Defects of Character
"Make a New Heart and a New Mind"

Are you really ready to have all these defects of character removed? Or put another way are you really ready "to make a new heart and a new mind"? The change we are entirely ready for is not a light-hearted change, but a deep fundamental change to our character and to our personality, a change deep within our heart. NA refers to this as a "complete personality change". But this change is really about a fundamental change in our heart. This shows we are in the process of becoming a brand-new person. One who will think and act differently than before. Step Six says to "remove all these defects of character" and so it is important to not hold on to any. It is important to not hold on to any defects that might put our recovery at risk of relapse, and it is important to not hold on to any defects that might hold us back from a fully restored relationship with God. It is only when we are entirely ready and willing for God to remove all our defects of character that we can have a complete personality change or that we can begin to have "a new heart and a new mind". It will not happen all at once, but it will be a gradual and obvious change. A change in your character and it will also lead to a deeper connection with God and a stronger faith in God as well. NA on page 346 brings many of these principles together when it states:

> "I went back to the Sixth Step and then worked the Seventh Step again. I needed more than a year to understand the choices made in Steps Six and Seven. These discoveries were the beginning of a new relationship with God."[55]

This final quote from NA is very similar to the Bible passage from Ezekiel 11:19 (GNT) that says:

> "I will give them a new heart and a new mind. I will take away their stubborn heart of stone and will give them an obedient heart."

This passage also indicates a dramatic change. Also, this passage and the message of Step Six is consistent with the recovery saying that "if nothing changes then nothing changes." This dramatic change is in our very nature, deep in our heart, such that God will "give them a new heart and a new mind and that God "will give them an obedient heart".

The main point of Step Six is for you to be "entirely ready" and entirely willing to have God do the spiritual surgery to remove your defects of character. It will not be fast or quick or easy and it will at times be painful. But as the Bible passage says the result is that God will "give them a new heart and a new mind".

Step Six of Recovery presents you with the question of are you "entirely ready and willing to have God remove all your defects of character?" Step Six is an important step and can be a dramatic step forward in your recovery and a dramatic step forward in your faith as well. Are you a ready and willing patient and are you ready for surgery? Do you yield yourself to God as the surgeon? And are you entirely willing to let God do the spiritual surgery removing all your character defects? Are you ready for a deep and fundamental change in your heart that leads you to think and act differently?

Embrace the message of the passage from Ezekiel 11:19 for yourself that says:

> "I will give them a new heart and a new mind. I will take away their stubborn heart of stone and will give them an obedient heart."

I pray you will allow God to work in your life removing all your character defects, such that God gives you "a new heart and a new mind".

Brief Summary of Step Six

"We were entirely ready to have God remove
all these defects of character."[56]
(Step Six from NA)

1) Were Entirely Ready
   a. "We were ready and willing for change."
2) Have God Remove
   a. "God will remove the defects not us".
3) Remove All Defects of Character
   a. "Make a new heart and a new mind".

Step Six:
Additional Bible Passages

Ezekiel 11:19 (GNT)

I will give them a new heart and a new mind.
I will take away their stubborn heart of stone and will
give them an obedient heart."

Psalm 118:24 (NKJV)

This *is* the day the Lord has made; We will rejoice and
be glad in it.

2 Corinthians 6:2 (NKJV)

For He says: "In an acceptable time I have heard you,
And in the day of salvation I have helped you." Behold,
now *is* the accepted time; behold, now *is* the day of
salvation.

Psalm 30:2 (NKJV)

O Lord my God, I cried out to You, And You healed
me.

2 Chronicles 7:14 (NIV)

If my people, who are called by my name, will humble
themselves and pray and seek my face and turn from
their wicked ways, then I will hear from heaven, and I
will forgive their sin and will heal their land.

Step Seven:
Humbly Ask God

"We humbly asked him to remove
our shortcomings."[57]
(Step Seven from NA)

=================================

"If we confess our sins, he is faithful
and just to forgive us our sins and to
cleanse us from all unrighteousness."
(1 John 1:9 ESV)

=================================

"We ask humbly, not in defeat, but with joyful
expectation that God will remove our
shortcomings in his timeframe."[58]
(The Hope Recovery Devotional)

=================================

This chapter is on Step Seven of Recovery which is given by Narcotics Anonymous as:

> "We humbly asked Him to remove our shortcomings."[59]

This Step Seven builds on the previous steps and especially on Step Six that says from NA:

> "We were entirely ready to have God remove all these defects of character."[60]

This Step Seven goes further than just being ready and willing to have God remove our defects of character. Now with Step Seven we ask God to begin this process. We ask God to remove our shortcomings. NA introduces Step Seven with these words on page 36:

> "Having decided that we want God to relieve us of the useless or destructive aspects of our personalities, we have arrived at the Seventh Step (and later...) By admitting this, we achieved a glimpse of humility."[61]

And later NA expands on this introduction and says:

> "The Seventh Step is an action step, and it is time to ask God for help and relief. We have to understand that our way of thinking is not the only way; other people can give us direction."[62]

So again, Step Seven from NA is given as:

"We humbly asked Him to remove our shortcomings."[63]

Let me suggest that there are four key principles for Step Seven of Recovery. And as with the other Steps as given by NA Step Seven also starts with "We" to emphasize that you are not alone and that you are part of a recovery community in your AA or NA groups, your faith-based groups, your church and your family and friends that support you and your recovery.

Humbly Ask
"We understand we need help"

The first principle here is that we humbly asked, as in "We understand we need help". It is not easy to ask for help. It may be quite humbling, but at this point in Step Seven it is absolutely the next right thing to do. We ask for help knowing that we cannot do it ourselves. We ask for help humbly, but not in defeat or in failure. We ask for help with a hopeful expectation that God will indeed help us. Step Seven is really a prayer, a simple prayer that begins with a sense of humility. We humbly pray and this humility is an important part of our personal growth as NA says on page 36:

> "This is the main ingredient of Step Seven. Humility is a result of getting honest with ourselves."[64]

In Step Seven we humbly ask for help because we know we need help and as we are truly honest with ourselves, we understand and accept that we need help. And so, in Step Seven "we humbly ask" for help.

Ask God
"We asked the one who is able to help"

It is important to ask for help and here we asked God, as in "We asked the one who is able to help." It is one thing to humbly ask for help, but it is important to ask the one who can actually help. Here in Step Seven, we humbly ask God for help, because God is absolutely the one who can help us. We ask God, because he is indeed the true "higher power". God is the "power greater than ourselves" and he is able to meet our needs and he is the right one for us to humbly ask for help.

Ask God to Remove
"To completely remove our
shortcomings and defects"

And here we asked God to remove, as in "to completely remove" our shortcomings and our defects. This is not a prayer asking God to help us manage our personal failings and defects, but to completely remove them. This is a simple honest prayer for God to begin the work to change us. To change our heart and mind so that we become the person of God that he intends us to be. This reminds me of the passage from 2 Corinthians 5:17 (NKJV) that says:

"Therefore, if anyone *is* in Christ, *he is* a new creation; old things have passed away; behold, all things have become new."

This is a great passage that indicates that with God in our life he will change us. As he works in our life, we will not be the same person, we will have a new heart and a new mind and we will think and act differently. Of course, this does not happen all at once, but it does start with an honest prayer, a simple honest prayer for God to completely remove our shortcomings and defects.

Ask God to Remove Our Shortcomings
"Remove any sinful way in our life"

Here we asked God to remove our shortcomings, as in "to remove any sinful way in our life". In this prayer of Step Seven, we humbly and wisely ask God to completely remove our shortcomings. This word "shortcomings" is another way of saying the "sin" in our life. Not all of our personal shortcomings and defects and failings are sinful. Many of them are sinful or, in the least, do not honor God. So the prayer here is asking God to completely remove our shortcomings, and this includes any sin in our life. Here in Step Seven, we humbly ask God to remove our shortcomings, to remove the sin in our life, to forgive us of our sin and to change us.

In Step Seven, God begins changing our heart and mind so that we become the person that God wants us to become. This prayer of Step Seven reminds me of a passage that I think relates well to this Step Seven and asking God to remove our shortcomings. This passage from 1 John 1: 9 (ESV) says:

> "If we confess our sins, he is faithful and just to forgive us our sins and to cleanse us from all unrighteousness."

This passage indicates we can have confidence that God will indeed forgive us of our sins and that he will also "cleanse us from all unrighteousness". This phrase of "cleanse us" suggests that God is purifying us and changing our hearts and minds to think and act differently and that God is indeed making us into new creations and changing us into the person of God that he wants us to become. This passage indicates that God is "faithful and just to forgive us our sins". I encourage you to apply this passage to yourself and to consider that God wants to forgive you and for you to accept God's forgiveness. Often, people in early recovery struggle with being able to accept God's forgiveness for all they have done in the past. Perhaps, you feel that way right now that you are not sure God will forgive you for all the harm and damage you have done to your loved ones in the past and maybe you don't even want to remember some of the things you have done. But I encourage you to remember this passage of 1 John1:9 that says God is "faithful and just to forgive you of your sins... and even to cleanse you from all unrighteousness."

Step Seven is the beginning of God changing you into the man or woman of God that he wants you to become. Embrace this step and accept God's forgiveness and be open to how God will move in your life to remove your shortcomings and defects one day at a time, and then be amazed at what God does in your life.

Brief Summary of Step Seven

"We humbly asked him to remove our shortcomings."[65]
(Step Seven from NA)

1) Humbly Ask
    a. "We understand we need help".
2) Ask God
    a. "We asked the one who is able to help".
3) Ask God to Remove
    a. "To completely remove our shortcomings and defects".
4) Ask God to Remove our Shortcomings
    a. "Remove any sinful way in our life".

Step Seven:
Additional Bible Passages

1 John 1:9 (ESV)
If we confess our sins, he is faithful and just to forgive us our sins and to cleanse us from all unrighteousness.

Psalm 18:6 (NKJV)
In my distress I called upon the Lord, And cried out to my God; He heard my voice from His temple, And my cry came before Him, *even* to His ears.

Psalm 34:17 (NIV)
The righteous cry out, and the Lord hears them; he delivers them from all their troubles.

1 Peter 5:6-8 (NIV)
Humble yourselves, therefore, under God's mighty hand, that he may lift you up in due time. [7] Cast all your anxiety on him because he cares for you.

2 Corinthians 5:17 (NKJV)
Therefore, if anyone *is* in Christ, *he is* a new creation; old things have passed away; behold, all things have become new.

Psalm 51:10 (ESV)
Create in me a clean heart, O God, and renew a right spirit within me.

"We made a list of all persons we had harmed,
and became willing to make amends
to them all."[66]
(Step Eight from NA)

==

"What a wretched man I am! Who will rescue
me from this body that is subject to death?
Thanks be to God, who delivers me through
Jesus Christ our Lord!"
(Romans 7:24-25)

==

"Step Eight will not be easy, but continue on
with the list of Step Eight and pray for God's
wisdom, guidance, and for relationships
to be restored."[67]
(The Hope Recovery Devotional)

==

This chapter is on Step Eight of Recovery, and it is again about making a list. Step Eight from Narcotics Anonymous is given as:

> "We made a list of all persons we had harmed, and became willing to make amends to them all."[68]

Step Eight is another step where we make a list. We do not actually make the amends in this step, but just make the list. As part of the introduction to Step Eight NA says this regarding the idea of "making a list" when it says on page 39:

> "The final difficulty in working the Eighth Step is separating it from the Ninth Step. Projections about actually making amends can be a major obstacle both in making the list and in becoming willing. We do this step as if there were no Ninth Step. We do not even think about making the amends but just concentrate on exactly what the Eighth Step says: make a list and become willing."[69]

Also, from AA in their introduction to Step Eight they bring out one of the spiritual components of Step Eight when they say on page 77:

> "At the moment we are trying to put our lives in order. But this is not an end in itself. Our real purpose is to fit ourselves to be of maximum service to God and the people about us."[70]

NA on page 38 brings out the point that Step Eight is not about us, but about others and how we hurt them in the past. To this NA says:

"By writing our list, we can no longer deny that we caused harm. We admit that we hurt others, directly or indirectly, through some action, lie, broken promise or neglect (and later...) We face this list honestly, and openly examine our faults so we can become willing to make amends."[71]

In Step Eight, we begin the process of restoring relationships with others. It is possible that some of these relationships won't be restored and that can be ok. But it is important to make the list of people we have harmed and to be willing to make the amends, with the focus always on the other person and not on ourselves. This step is not about the people who have harmed us, or have hurt us, but Step Eight is only about the people we have harmed and the people we have hurt. So, again Step Eight from NA reads as:

"We made a list of all persons we had harmed, and became willing to make amends to them all."[72]

I suggest that there are three key principles for Step Eight of Recovery, and as with the other Steps, Step Eight emphasizes you are not alone in your recovery by starting with the word "We". It reminds us you are part of a recovery community. But that means that you must take steps to join and participate in recovery groups and be intentional in building a recovery community. So, I encourage you to make AA, NA, and faith-based groups a part of your regular weekly schedule in addition to a home church as well.

Made a List
"Actually made an honest and complete list"

Here in Step Eight, we made a list, as in "we actually made an honest and complete list". Here we do not actually make amends, we just make the list. It is often recommended to not even think about actually making the amends, but just create the list. As NA says, make this list, as if Step Nine does not even exist. Here in Step Eight, the focus is only on making a complete and honest list of people we have harmed or people we have hurt is some way. So do not focus on what making the amends might actually look like, but simply focus on making the amends list. On a practical note, I encourage you to actually make a list and to document it on a notepad, or a computer, or your phone. Actually create your list in some way.

Made a List of Persons We Have Harmed
"It is not about us"

Here we made a list of all persons we have harmed, as in "It is not about us, but about the people we have harmed". Step Eight will be a really tough and challenging step, because the natural tendency is for us to think first about how we were harmed and about how we were hurt or offended. The tendency might be to rationalize that we would not have done what we did if the other person had not done something to us first. It is also important to note that Step Eight is not about making a list to make people like us again. It is only about making a list of people we have harmed and then being willing to make the amends.

This Step Eight list will likely be pretty revealing for us as we see how many people we have actually harmed. It may be quite powerful to see this list in a written or typed document. This list will likely be pretty convincing of how terrible we were in our addicted past and one of the outcomes might be that we are perhaps now a more forgiving person for the people who may have harmed us in the past or even in the future as well.

Became Willing to Make Amends
"Putting other above ourselves"

This is a big step as we became willing to make amends, as in "we were putting others above ourselves". This change shows "an internal heart change" and it is because of this internal heart change that we seek to honor God. We seek now to do the right thing and part of that right thing is putting others before ourselves. We become willing to put the needs of others before our own. In Step Eight we are putting the needs of others, the ones we have harmed, before our own needs and we then become willing to make amends. The passage from Philippians 2:3 reflects this heart change when it states:

"Do nothing out of selfish ambition or vain conceit. Rather, in humility value others above yourselves."

Step Eight is all about putting the needs of others above our own needs. Step Eight is a powerful step, but as you create this list for yourself, of all the people you have harmed, it may be overwhelming. You may find that this list is a very long list, and it includes many terrible harms that you have done to others, even to friends and loved ones. You may feel that you are a very bad person, perhaps even a terrible person. You may feel that you are beyond God's grace and mercy and beyond God's forgiveness. But fortunately, the Bible tells a different story of God's grace and mercy as is reflected in the passage from Romans 7:24-25 (NIV) where it seems as if the apostle Paul has just completed a Step Eight list for himself as he says:

> "What a wretched man I am! Who will rescue me from this body that is subject to death? [25] Thanks be to God, who delivers me through Jesus Christ our Lord!"

While you may feel that the first part of the passage is true for you, that you are "a wretched" person. I encourage you to read the entire passage. Yes, you and I and really everyone, without God, are "wretched" people; people that need being "rescued". Fortunately, this passage does not leave us without hope, but it tells us that "Thanks be to God" we are rescued by grace through faith in the Lord Jesus Christ and what he has done for us. I encourage you to embrace this message of hope and to accept God's forgiveness and to accept his grace and mercy, so that you can have a true internal heart change. This internal heart change, that seeks to honor God in all you do, and that includes putting the needs of others before your own needs.

Step Eight is a powerful step that can help you put the needs of others before your own needs and it can help you keep the focus off yourself and on others and on God as well. Step Eight can indeed be a big step forward that reflects an internal heart change. An internal heart change where you seek to honor God in all you do, and part of that heart change is by putting the needs of others before your own. Start today as you reflect this internal heart change for yourself as you seek to honor God in all you do by putting others before yourself.

Brief Summary of Step Eight

"We made a list of all persons we had harmed, and became willing to make amends to them all."[73]
(Step Eight from NA)

1) Made a List
   a. "Actually made an honest and complete list."
2) Made a List of Persons We Have Harmed
   a. "It is not about us".
3) Became Willing to Make Amends
   a. "Putting others above ourselves".

Step Eight:
Additional Bible Passages

Romans 7:24-25 (NIV)
What a wretched man I am! Who will rescue me from this body that is subject to death? Thanks be to God, who delivers me through Jesus Christ our Lord!

Philippians 2:3-4 (ESV)
Do nothing from selfish ambition or conceit, but in humility count others more significant than yourselves. [4] Let each of you look not only to his own interests, but also to the interests of others.

Ephesians 4:32 (NIV)
Be kind and compassionate to one another, forgiving each other, just as in Christ God forgave you.

John 15:12 (NIV)
My command is this: Love each other as I have loved you.

Luke 6:27-28 (ESV)
But I say to you who hear, Love your enemies, do good to those who hate you, [28] bless those who curse you, pray for those who abuse you.

Step Nine:
Made Amends Wherever Possible

"We made direct amends to such people
wherever possible, except when to do so
would injure them or others."[74]
(Step Nine from NA)

================================

"But Zacchaeus stood up and said to the Lord,
'Look, Lord! Here and now I give half of my
possessions to the poor, and if I have cheated
anybody out of anything, I will pay back four
times the amount.' [9]Jesus said to him, "Today
salvation has come to this house".
(Luke 19:8-9 NIV)

================================

"We need to be humble and sensitive
to the other person and only make the amends
if it will not injure them or others."[75]
(The Hope Recovery Devotional)

================================

This chapter is on Step Nine of Recovery, which continues the focus on a heart change and thinking of others before ourselves. Step Nine from Narcotics Anonymous is given as:

"We made direct amends to such people wherever possible, except when to do so would injure them or others."[76]

Step Nine really highlights one of the fundamental principles of The Twelve Steps of Recovery in that at the core of The Twelve Steps the focus is on a heart change, a heart change that involves a deep personality change. The Twelve Steps are focused on dramatic change that begins with a spiritual change and this involves a newfound relationship with God, with our higher power. This new relationship with God then also impacts how we think and act and ultimately it also impacts our relationship with people, with our friends and loved ones, and co-workers, and even to everyone we interact with. This focus of The Twelve Steps of Recovery is evident throughout each step. The Twelve Steps are all integrated with careful and intentional reflection at each step along the way. They are not simply a list of action steps, but they are combined with careful and intentional reflection before any action steps are taken. These action steps include words of instruction such as 'we admitted, came to believe, made a decision, searching and fearless, exact nature, were entirely ready, humbly asked, and became willing'. These are words that require careful consideration and reflection at each step along the way of The Twelve

Steps of Recovery. They all focus on a heart change and a deep personality change. In essence, a spiritual change that reflects a newfound relationship with God, that then causes us to change how we interact with our family and friends, and even how we interact with all people each and every day. All of this brings us to Step Nine of Recovery, which after all of this heart change, and personality change, and spiritual change, now we are given the instruction to make amends. We are now to actually go and make amends to the people we have harmed. But, even Step Nine keeps the focus on other people as part of the instruction is to do so "wherever possible... except when to do so would injure them or others". Yes, it is important to make amends to those we have harmed, but the focus still requires us to carefully and intentionally consider if the amends would injure them or others. Likely, this is a dramatic change for many of us from our past way of living.

As part of the introduction to Step Nine NA says this on page 40:

> "We want to be free of our guilt, but we don't wish to do so at the expense of anyone else. We might run the risk of involving a third person or some companion from our using days who does not wish to be exposed. We do not have the right or the need to endanger another person."[77]

Yes, it is important to make the amends, if possible, but it is also equally important to consider if it will injure someone else in the process. NA speaks about Step Nine from a broad perspective when they state on page 41:

"Sometimes the only way we can make amends is to contribute to society. Now, we are helping ourselves and other addicts to recover. This is a tremendous amend to the whole community."[78]

Here NA points out, in their own way, that the most important thing we can do for ourselves and other addicts and even for the whole community is to be successful in recovery. Being successful in recovery is a great amend to everyone! NA ends their introduction to Step Nine when they point out the spiritual component of Step Nine on page 42 when they say:

"A lot of courage and faith goes into making an amend, and a lot of spiritual growth results."[79]

Again, Step Nine from NA reads as:

"We made direct amends to such people wherever possible, except when to do so would injure them or others."[80]

I suggest that there are three key principles for Step Nine of Recovery.

Made Direct Amends
"We made specific amends
for a specific harm"

Here we made direct amends, as in "we made specific amends for a specific harm." The amends of Step Nine are not intended to be a general expression of remorse. It is not intended to be a message of "I'm sorry for everything". But it is intended to be a specific amends for a specific harm. A specific amends for a specific harm that was done to the person we are making the amends to and if possible, the amends should be proportional to the harm we caused. It is also important for Step Nine that we keep the focus on making the amends. We are not there to argue, or to explain, or to rationalize why we did what we did. We are there to simply and humbly make amends to them! It is also important to remember that we cannot control how people will respond. But we can control how we plan and prepare before we make the amends. I suggest you pray before you go to make the amends. Pray for a humble spirit and for the ability to present the amends in a way that is most appropriate for the other person and then to make the amends in a humble and compassionate manner.

To Such Persons Wherever Possible
"Make specific amends to specific people"

Here we made amends to such persons wherever possible, as in "make specific amends to specific people". In Step Nine, we make specific amends to specific people, to the specific people we have harmed. This is again all about being specific and intentional and even a specific time of meeting together. This is typically a one-on-one meeting and an in-person meeting, and it will likely be difficult. But while it will likely be difficult, it could also be a wonderful time of restoration. Often, relationships are restored in ways that might be unexpected. As Step Nine is very much about being specific, I suggest that you carefully consider when and where you meet. You should be sensitive to make it at a time and place that is most appropriate for the other person. Then I would also suggest that you carefully consider the words you will use to express your amends in a way that is truthful, but also that might be the most sensitive and caring to the other person as well.

Unless It Would Injure Them or Others
"Don't make it worse"

Principle three brings in the perspective that the amends should be done, unless to do so would injure them or others, or in other words "don't make it worse". Step Nine is all about making amends to the person we had harmed, but we need to be careful to not make matters worse! Making amends is good for us, but we need to also be careful that it does not cause more harm. Here we need to prayerfully consider the amends of Step Nine. We need to pray for wisdom and, if necessary, seek wise counsel from a trusted friend, or sponsor, or pastor before making the amends, because the last thing we want to do is to make matters worse by making our amends. Here, we need to be compassionate and consider the needs and feelings of the other person. Likely that is very different from how we felt and acted when we first caused the harm. This type of consideration reflects a personality change, a heart change, and ultimately of a spiritual change as well, which is what The Twelve Steps of Recovery are all about.

This discussion of Step Nine reminds me of the passage from Luke 19:8-9, which I think relates well to the principles of Step Nine when it talks about repaying for past harms and then even dramatic change as well. Luke 19:8-9 (NIV) states:

> "But Zacchaeus stood up and said to the Lord, 'Look, Lord! Here and now I give half of my possessions to the poor, and if I have cheated anybody out of anything, I will pay back four times the amount.' [9] Jesus said to him, "Today salvation has come to this house, because this man, too, is a son of Abraham."

Zacchaeus was viewed by most people as a sinner, as he was over charging for taxes for his own benefit. But Jesus had kindly engaged with Zacchaeus, and Jesus said he wanted to visit at his house that evening. Zacchaeus was so moved by this expression of kindness, grace, and compassion that Zacchaeus made this great declaration to correct the harm he had caused to anyone that he had "cheated" and that he would "pay back four times the amount". What a great example of making an amends for the harm he had caused. Jesus wanted Zacchaeus to have a restored relationship with God. Jesus was sensitive and compassionate to Zacchaeus, and Zacchaeus responded in a dramatic way.

Step Nine is a powerful step where the focus is on others and making specific amends for the specific harm, we had caused someone else and doing it in a way that is compassionate and sensitive to that person.

As I consider Step Nine of Recovery, I am so grateful that God does not require that of us. God does not require us to make amends to him for all our past sin, for all the past times we failed God, but all that God requires is an expression of faith in Christ and for us to put our hope and faith and trust in Jesus. In a sense, Jesus made the ultimate "amends" for all of us. Jesus paid our amends on the cross such that all we need to do is to accept the amends that he provided for us. While that is difficult to understand, it is a clear message of the Bible. So, I encourage you to accept the great "amends" that Jesus provided on the cross. John 3:16 (NIV) expresses God's great love for us and even this great "amends" when it states:

> "For God so loved the world that he gave his one and only Son, that whoever believes in him shall not perish but have eternal life."

I encourage you to consider Step Nine carefully when you prepare to make your amends and do it with kindness, grace, and compassion and in a way that is sensitive to the person you are making the amends to, and then be specific with your amends, to specific people and with a humble and caring spirit.

And I ask you to consider accepting the "ultimate amends" that God made for you and for everyone. It was because of God's great love for you and for the world, that he gave his one and only Son to provide the free gift of his "amends" of what Jesus did on the cross for you and for me and for everyone.

Brief Summary of Step Nine

"We made direct amends to such people wherever possible, except when to do so would injure them or others."[81]
(Step Nine from NA)

1) Made Direct Amends
    a. "We made specific amends for a specific harm."
2) To Such Persons Wherever Possible
    a. "Make specific amends to specific people".
3) Unless It Would Injure Them or Others
    a. "Don't make it worse".

Step Nine:
Additional Bible Passages

Luke 19:8-9 NIV
But Zacchaeus stood up and said to the Lord, "Look, Lord! Here and now I give half of my possessions to the poor, and if I have cheated anybody out of anything, I will pay back four times the amount." [9]Jesus said to him, "Today salvation has come to this house.

Galatians 6:10 (NKJV)
Therefore, as we have opportunity, let us do good to all, especially to those who are of the household of faith.

Hebrews 13:16 (NKJV)
But do not forget to do good and to share, for with such sacrifices God is well pleased.

Ephesians 4:32 (NKJV)
And be kind to one another, tenderhearted, forgiving one another, even as God in Christ forgave you.

Luke 23:34 (NIV)
Jesus said, "Father, forgive them, for they do not know what they are doing." And they divided up his clothes by casting lots.

"We continued to take personal inventory and when we were wrong promptly admitted it."[82]
(Step Ten from NA)

==================================

"If we say that we have no sin, we deceive ourselves, and the truth is not in us.
If we confess our sins, He is faithful and just to forgive us our sins and to cleanse us from all unrighteousness."
(1 John 1:8-9 NKJV)

==================================

"Bring our sins and personal failures to God and ask him for forgiveness and guidance so we do not fall into those same sins again."[83]
(The Hope Recovery Devotional)

==================================

This chapter is on Step Ten of Recovery where we are instructed to continue to take personal inventory. Step Ten of Recovery from Narcotics Anonymous is given as:

> "We continued to take personal inventory and when we were wrong promptly admitted it."[84]

Step Ten begins to take us in a different direction from the previous several steps. Step Ten suggests a "continued" or even daily process of recovery. In their introduction to Step Ten AA suggests this is not a once and done process, but a daily process and one that lasts for our lifetime. So, on page 84 AA says:

> "This thought brings us to *Step Ten,* which suggests we continue to take personal inventory and continue to set right any new mistakes as we go along. We vigorously commenced this way of living as we cleaned up the past. We have entered the world of the Spirit. Our next function is to grow in understanding and effectiveness. This is not an overnight matter. It should continue for our lifetime."[85]

And NA in their introduction to Step Ten speaks about Step Ten in a broad perspective and shows just how important Step Ten can be as a brand-new way of living when it states on page 42:

"We need to remember that everyone makes mistakes. We will never be perfect. However, we can accept ourselves by using Step Ten. By continuing a personal inventory, we are set free, in the here and now, from ourselves and the past. We no longer justify our existence. This step allows us to be ourselves."[86]

This quote indicates that we acknowledge we will make "mistakes" and that we "will never be perfect" and that is all ok. But, with Step Ten we take a personal inventory to address any concerns now, right away before they become a problem for us or others. And really this is a relief as it removes the pressure of life and as NA says: Step Ten helps to set us "free... in the here and now"!

So, Step Ten from NA reads:

"We continued to take personal inventory and when we were wrong promptly admitted it."[87]

In my view there are four key principles for Step Ten of Recovery.

We Continued Every Day
"It is a daily process not once and done"

The main point here is that we continued every day as in "It is a daily process not once and done."

Step Ten is to be done each and every day. It is not something that is done once and then we are all done, forever. Rather, "we continued" indicates it is an ongoing process. By continuing to do Step Ten every day it helps us. It helps us to build new routines, and new habits that are positive for us and positive for our recovery and even positive for those around us. NA speaks to this daily process on page 43 when it says:

> "The Tenth Step can be a pressure relief valve. We work this step while the day's ups and downs are still fresh in our minds. We list what we have done and try not to rationalize our actions. This may be done in writing at the end of the day."[88]

This daily process is another sign that there is a spiritual change taking place and that we are looking beyond ourselves and are trying to be respectful of others and even to honor God by doing the next right thing.

Take Personal Inventory
"Consider where we failed God or others"

The second principle of Step Ten is to take personal inventory, as in "To consider where we failed God or others." This daily process of Step Ten also includes taking time for thoughtful and careful reflection, so that we can accurately assess our thoughts, and words, and actions where we might have harmed someone or failed God or others in some way. Just as with so many other steps of The Twelve Steps of Recovery, Step Ten also requires thoughtful and careful reflection in order to do Step Ten properly.

Recognize Our Wrongs
"Recognize our wrongs and accept them"

The third principle of Step Ten is to recognize our wrongs, or in other words "To recognize our wrongs and accept them." This means that we see our own wrongs for what they are and acknowledge that we were wrong. Our wrong was not because of someone else and what they did. It was because we did the wrong thing or said the wrong thing or perhaps even just thought the wrong thing. In essence this means we did not rationalize our wrongs away. We did not make excuses, but we recognized our wrong and accepted it. We recognize that we were responsible for it and not someone else or some other exceptional set of circumstances. We were wrong and we accepted it.

Promptly Admit Our Wrongs
"Humbly confess our wrongs and our sins"

The fourth and final principle of Step Ten is to promptly admit our wrongs, as in "To humbly confess our wrongs and our sins." This is an action that should be prompt, but also should be done humbly. It is important to admit our wrongs for sure, but we need to do it with a spirit of humility. Whether we are admitting our wrongs to someone we had wronged or even if we are confessing our sins to God, humility needs to be a part of this process. This is also an indication of growth in our recovery and growth in our spiritual life as well. AA speaks to this spiritual aspect of Step Ten when it says on page 85:

> "We are neither cocky nor are we afraid. That is our experience. That is how we react so long as we keep in fit spiritual condition. (and later...) If we have carefully followed directions, we have begun to sense the flow of His Spirit into us. To some extent we have become God-conscious. We have begun to develop this vital sixth sense."[89]

This quote indicates the importance of a spiritual experience with God. Both books of AA and NA clearly show the importance of the spiritual component of recovery and of life as well. Step Ten is important, but it requires a humble spirit, and it requires thoughtful and careful reflection of our personal inventory that really can only be successful if we allow God to direct our inspection of our personal inventory.

Step Ten and this aspect of admitting our wrongs and to do it with a humble spirit reminds me of Psalm 139:23-24 where it says:

> "Search me, God, and know my heart; test me and know my anxious thoughts. [24] See if there is any offensive way in me, and lead me in the way everlasting."

To do Step Ten properly, we need to have God a part of the process. We need to have God do the searching of our heart and mind to reveal "any offensive way in us". And then this searching of our heart, or the searching of our personal inventory, led by God, will bring us face to face with this basic truth as we are told in 1 John 1:8-9 (ESV) where it says:

> "If we say we have no sin, we deceive ourselves, and the truth is not in us. [9] If we confess our sins, he is faithful and just to forgive us our sins and to cleanse us from all unrighteousness."

As we let God do the searching of our personal inventory, we will see the wrongs in our life, we will see the sin in our life, and thankfully this passage tells us to confess our sins, and that God is faithful and just and will forgive us of all our sins! This passage from 1 John 1:8-9 is really quite comforting, as we know, we are not perfect. We will make mistakes and we will sin, but this passage tells us that God "is faithful and just to forgive us our sins" and even more he will "cleans us from all unrighteousness." What a comforting message, what a great assurance that God will forgive us! This is not only a comforting message as we do a personal inventory every day, but it is a comforting message to know that God will forgive us or all of our past sins as well!

I encourage you to embrace this truth of the Bible for you for today and even for your past sins, regardless of what you might have done in the past. God does indeed want to forgive you. Start today and bring all of your past sins and failings to God and he will indeed forgive you and cleans you from all unrighteousness!

Brief Summary of Step Ten

"We continued to take personal inventory and when we were wrong promptly admitted it."[90]
(Step Ten from NA)

1) We Continued Every Day
    a. "It is a daily process not once and done."
2) Take Personal Inventory
    a. "Consider where we failed God or others."
3) Recognize Our Wrongs
    a. "Recognize our wrongs and accept them."
4) Promptly Admit Our Wrongs
    a. "Humbly confess our wrongs and our sins."

Step Ten:
Additional Bible Passages

1 John 1:8-9 NKJV
If we say that we have no sin, we deceive ourselves, and the truth is not in us. If we confess our sins, He is faithful and just to forgive us our sins and to cleanse us from all unrighteousness.

Mark 1:35 (NIV)
Very early in the morning, while it was still dark, Jesus got up, left the house and went off to a solitary place, where he prayed.

Micah 6:8 (ESV)
He has told you, O man, what is good; and what does the Lord require of you but to do justice, and to love kindness, and to walk humbly with your God?

Colossians 3:13 (NIV)
Bear with each other and forgive one another if any of you has a grievance against someone. Forgive as the Lord forgave you.

Philippians 4:6 (NKJV)
Be anxious for nothing, but in everything by prayer and supplication, with thanksgiving, let your requests be made known to God;

Step Eleven:
Through Prayer and Meditation

"We sought through prayer and meditation to improve our conscious contact with God as we understood Him, praying only for knowledge of His will for us and the power to carry that out.[91]
(Step Eleven from NA)

====================================

"Pray then like this: "Our Father in heaven, hallowed be your name. [10] Your kingdom come, your will be done, on earth as it is in heaven."
Matthew (6:9-10 ESV)

====================================

"This new prayer of Step Eleven
takes the focus off of us and on to God
and his will in our life."[92]
(The Hope Recovery Devotional)

====================================

This chapter on Step Eleven of Recovery highlights, in many ways, the importance of the spiritual component of The Twelve Steps. And the wording used in Step Eleven very much depicts a faith-based perspective of The Twelve Steps as well. Step Eleven from Narcotics Anonymous states:

> "We sought through prayer and meditation to improve our conscious contact with God as we understood Him, praying only for knowledge of His will for us and the power to carry that out."[93]

Step Eleven is really a foundational step not only for recovery but also for growing in our faith as well. This step also indicates it should be a daily process as an everyday event. NA and AA both indicate that Step Eleven is very much focused on seeking God's will in our life and not our own will and that this new focus is very important for success in recovery and for growing deeper in our faith as well.

NA introduces the Eleventh step on page 45 when it says:

> "The more we improve our conscious contact with our God through prayer and meditation, the easier it is to say, 'Your will, not mine, be done.' We can ask for God's help when we need it, and our lives get better."[94]

AA presents a similar focus regarding Step Eleven when they say on pages 87:

"As we go through the day we pause, when agitated or doubtful, and ask for the right thought or action. We constantly remind ourselves we are no longer running the show, humbly saying to ourselves many times each day "Thy will be done.""[95]

So again, Step Eleven from NA reads:

"We sought through prayer and meditation to improve our conscious contact with God as we understood Him, praying only for knowledge of His will for us and the power to carry that out."[96]

I'd like to suggest there are four key principles for Step Eleven of Recovery.

Sought Through Prayer and Meditation
"We made the decision to pray and meditate"

The initial focus is on the commitment for prayer and meditation or put another way "we made the decision to pray and meditate". This first principle shows it is an intentional decision to take time to pray and to meditate. It is a conscious decision to schedule time every day to pray and meditate. It is not an occasional or sporadic event of prayer, but it is an intentional decision to take time to pray and to meditate. It is interesting that this Eleventh Step also includes the idea of meditation. Meditation adds the aspect of pausing and listening for God's response to our prayer and to be patient and take time to listen for the still quiet voice of God as he might direct us.

Improve Our Conscious Contact with God
"Draw close to God"

The second principle of Step Eleven is to improve our conscious contact with God, as in "To draw close to God". To draw close to God is to understand more and more about God and to nurture this close spiritual relationship with God. And as we understand more about God, I believe we will be more and more humbled before an amazing and merciful God that we will want, even more, to honor him in all we do. Faith is all about a spiritual relationship with God and a big part of that is for us to nurture this relationship with God and when we do seek to draw close to God, he will indeed respond.

The Bible verse of James 4:8 (NKJV) describes this relationship with God when it states:

"Draw near to God and He will draw near to you."

Pray for the Knowledge of God's Will
"Praying for God's will and not our own"

The third principle of Step Eleven is praying only for knowledge of God's will in our life, as in "Praying for God's will and not our own". This part of Step Eleven brings out the important principle that we are not praying for our own wants and needs and personal desires, but that we are praying for God's will in our life. We are not praying in a self-centered way of things for ourselves that we "think" might make our life better, but we are praying specifically for God's will in our life whatever that might be. This type of prayer really does reflect growth in our recovery and in our life as well. It is a prayer that genuinely seeks to know God's will and to put God's will first; to put God's will before our own wants and needs and personal desires. The beginning of the Lords' Prayer reflects this perspective when it states in Matthew 6:9-10 (NKJV):

> "Our Father in heaven, Hallowed be Your name.
> [10] Your kingdom come. Your will be done
> On earth as *it is* in heaven."

What a great connection of Step Eleven with The Lord's Prayer, as they both have the focus on God's will in our life.

Look to God's Power
"Rely on God's Power to do his will"

The fourth and final principle of Step Eleven is to look to God's power, as in "to rely on God's power to do his will". By now we fully understand that it is only with God's power that we can do anything. It is only with God's power that we can be successful in recovery, and it is only with God's power that we can carry out his will in our life. From step one of admitting we were powerless over our addiction and Step Two that we "came to believe that a Power greater than ourselves could restore us to sanity" and now to Step Eleven where it is the power of God and not our own power that can enable us to carry out his will in our life.

I encourage you to rely on God's power in your life and to do his will. It is easy to fall back into thinking we can do it ourselves in our own power, but that is why it is important to daily seek "through prayer and meditation to improve our conscious contact with God" so that we will be reminded each day to draw close to God and to seek his will and to rely on his power in our life.

Step Eleven brings several points into focus that it is only through prayer and meditation that we can draw close to God and this daily process will help us know his will for our life and that we need to rely on God's power to do his will. It is with these principles of Step Eleven we can be successful in recovery, grow in our faith, and that we can begin to see the purpose and plan that God has for us. It is with Step Eleven we can begin to see what God's will really is for us.

The full passage of The Lord's Prayer seems to expand on just what this Eleventh Step is all about to pray to our heavenly father to know his will for our basic needs every day, forgiveness of our sins, mercy to others, and the power to resist temptation as Matthew 6:9-13 (NKJV) states:

"Our Father in heaven, Hallowed be Your name.
[10] Your kingdom come. Your will be done

On earth as *it is* in heaven. [11] Give us this day our daily bread. [12] And forgive us our debts, As we forgive our debtors. [13] And do not lead us into temptation, But deliver us from the evil one."

I encourage you today, regardless of where you are at in recovery or in any struggle of life or even wherever you are at in your faith, to decide to schedule time every day to pray and meditate. It is ok if this is just a brief time for prayer and meditation and perhaps even a brief Bible reading as well. But decide to spend some time each day where you draw close to God and seek his will in your life. As you draw close to God, you will grow stronger in your faith and stronger with God's power in your life to carry out his will in your life and not your own.

Brief Summary of Step Eleven

"We sought through prayer and meditation to improve our conscious contact with God as we understood Him, praying only for knowledge of His will for us and the power to carry that out.[97]
(Step Eleven from NA)

1) Sought Through Prayer and Meditation
   a. "We made the decision to pray and meditate."
2) Improve Our Conscious Contact with God
   a. "Draw close to God".
3) Pray for Knowledge of God's Will
   a. "Praying for God's will and not our own".
4) Look to God's Power
   a. "Rely on God's power to do his will".

Step Eleven:
Additional Bible Passages

Matthew (6:9-10 ESV)
Pray then like this: "Our Father in heaven, hallowed be your name. [10] Your kingdom come, your will be done, on earth as it is in heaven.

James 4:8 (NKJV)
Draw near to God and He will draw near to you. Cleanse *your* hands, *you* sinners; and purify *your* hearts, *you* double-minded.

1 Chronicles 16:11 (NKJV)
Seek the Lord and His strength; Seek His face evermore!

1 Thessalonians 5:16-18 (NIV)
Rejoice always, [17] pray continually, [18] give thanks in all circumstances; for this is God's will for you in Christ Jesus.

Luke 9:23 (NKJV)
Then He said to *them* all, "If anyone desires to come after Me, let him deny himself, and take up his cross daily, and follow Me.

Matthew 6:33 (NKJV)
But seek first the kingdom of God and his righteousness, and all these things will be added to you.

Step Twelve:
Had a Spiritual Awakening

"Having had a spiritual awakening as a result of these steps, we tried to carry this message to addicts, and to practice these principles in all our affairs."[98]
(Step Twelve from NA)

==

"Jesus answered and said to him, "Most assuredly, I say to you, unless one is born again, he cannot see the kingdom of God."
(John 3:3 NKJV)

==

"And it is with this spiritual awakening we now have God in our life to help us day by day to practice these principles in all areas of our life."[99]
(The Hope Recovery Devotional)

==

This chapter is on Step Twelve of Recovery and the acknowledgment that you have had a "spiritual awakening". Step Twelve from Narcotics Anonymous states:

> "Having had a spiritual awakening as a result of these steps, we tried to carry this message to addicts, and to practice these principles in all our affairs."[100]

It is interesting what AA and NA selected for the very last and final step of The Twelve Steps of Recovery. They could have said many things as the final step, but they chose this statement and specific wording for Step Twelve as the final step. I think what they selected for Step Twelve also says much about what AA and NA feel are the key principles of the Twelve Steps of Recovery and ultimately what they feel are critical to success in recovery.

AA in their chapter on Step Twelve highlights what they feel is one of the most important aspects of The Twelve Steps of recovery when they state on page 99:

> "Remind the prospect that his recovery is not dependent upon people. It is dependent upon his relationship with God (and later...) Both you and the new man must walk day by day in the path of spiritual progress."[101]

In the NA introduction to Step Twelve they also emphasize the spiritual component as critical to recovery when they state on page 49:

> "The steps lead to an awakening of a spiritual nature. This awakening is evidenced by changes in our lives. These changes make us better able to live by spiritual principles and to carry our message of recovery and hope to the addict who still suffers."[102]

The importance of a spiritual change is quite clear for both AA and NA. To be successful in recovery, AA and NA indicate a spiritual change must take place. So, restating Step Twelve from NA reads:

> "Having had a spiritual awakening as a result of these steps, we tried to carry this message to addicts, and to practice these principles in all our affairs."[103]

Let me note this NA Step Twelve is the only step that does not begin with the word "We", but it still indicates a recovery community and still indicates you are not alone in your recovery and that in fact you are now the one reaching out to other addicts and alcoholics.

Let me suggest there are four key principles for Step Twelve of Recovery.

Had a Spiritual Awakening
"A restored relationship with God"

The first few words of Step Twelve acknowledge we had a spiritual awakening, or in other words we now have "a restored relationship with God". This "spiritual awakening" is all about a restored relationship with God. Before the Twelve Steps our spiritual life was dead or dormant or asleep, such that a "spiritual awakening" of some type was absolutely necessary and here in Step Twelve we are really acknowledging that yes, we have made a spiritual change. We now have a restored relationship with God; we are now living life differently with this "spiritual awakening". We now live each day seeking to honor God by doing the next right thing and that certainly starts with being clean and sober. This "spiritual awakening" of Step Twelve relates well to the passage of John 3:3 (NKJV) and the need for a spiritual change when it states:

> "Jesus answered and said to him, "Most assuredly, I say to you, unless one is born again, he cannot see the kingdom of God."

To be "born again" means being "born again spiritually" or in the words of Step Twelve having a "spiritual awakening". This simply means making a decision or making an expression of faith in God. There is no magic formula for this expression of faith. All that is required is a genuine expression of faith in God, by grace through faith in the Lord Jesus Christ and with that you will indeed begin your "spiritual awakening" to a brand-new restored relationship with God.

As a Result of These Steps
"This change is from working the steps and not a random happening"

The second principle of Step Twelve is the awareness that this dramatic spiritual change is a result of the Twelve Steps, as in "this change is from working the steps and not a random happening". This dramatic "spiritual change" did not just happen by chance; this dramatic change in your personality and how you think, and act did not just happen by some random chance event, but it happened because you followed The Twelve Steps of Recovery. You did the work necessary for a deep spiritual change or a "spiritual awakening", such that you began to have a fundamental personality change, a deep change in your values and in your heart and mind. And it is significant to note again, that these Twelve Steps of Recovery are rooted in biblical principles as well and that by working the steps it will naturally lead to a "spiritual awakening" and a restored relationship with God.

Carry this Message to Other Addicts
"Share the message of recovery and faith with others.

The third principle of Step Twelve is we try to carry this message to other addicts, as in "we share the message of recovery and of faith with others". To those that are in the midst of the addiction struggle, the primary message is one of recovery, which includes the message of hope, along with any help or encouragement possible in a caring, compassionate manner. But The Twelve Steps of Recovery also bring in the spiritual component and the need for God. So, at some point, the message of God and a "higher power" or a "spiritual awakening" should also be included as part of the message to carry to the addict or alcoholic. It is also important to share this spiritual message and this message of God in a way and at a time that is most appropriate for them to hear it and to receive it.

Practice These Principles in All Our Affairs
"Use these biblical principles
in all aspects of our life"

The fourth and final principle of Step Twelve is to practice these principles in all our affairs, as in "to use these biblical principles in all aspects of our life". The Twelve Steps of Recovery are based on biblical principles, and they are helpful not only for recovery but even for all aspects of life. What this means is to bring God into our everyday life as well. Certainly, God will give us guidance and wisdom and strength for the difficult issues and challenges of life, but God will give us guidance and wisdom and strength even for the everyday issues of life as well. God wants us to simply draw close to him and to seek him and to trust him. In many ways that is what Step Twelve and really all The Twelve Steps of Recovery are all about. They are about "trusting God" and yielding to his will in our life. Having a "spiritual awakening" and practicing these principles in all our affairs ultimately is about "trusting God and seeking to honor God in all we do.

While Step Twelve is the final step of The Twelve Steps of Recovery, it is certainly not the end of the steps, as these Twelve Steps are indeed solid principles for recovery and life as well. These principles are all built upon biblical principles of a "spiritual awakening" or a spiritual change and even transformation of your personality and your mind and heart, too. Recovery is still one day at a time, but now you have the true "higher power" to help you.

I encourage you today to embrace this message of Step Twelve and of a "spiritual awakening" and to draw close to God as never before, and to trust God with your recovery and to trust God even with your everyday events of life as well. And then to continue sharing this wonderful message of recovery and faith with so many others that are still searching for help and for hope and now you have a wonderful message of recovery and faith to share with others.

Brief Summary of Step Twelve

"Having had a spiritual awakening as a result
of these steps, we tried to carry this message
to addicts, and to practice these principles
in all our affairs."[104]
(Step Twelve from NA)

1) Had a Spiritual Awakening
   a. "A restored relationship with God".
2) As a Result of These Steps
   a. "This change is from working the steps, not a random happening".
3) Carry this Message to Other Addicts
   a. "Share the message of recovery and of faith with others".
4) Practice These Principles in All Our Affairs
   a. "Use these biblical principles in all aspects of our life".

Step Twelve:
Additional Bible Passages

(John 3:3 NKJV)
Jesus answered and said to him, "Most assuredly, I say to you, unless one is born again, he cannot see the kingdom of God.

John 3:16 (NIV)
For God so loved the world that he gave his one and only Son, that whoever believes in him shall not perish but have eternal life.

2 Corinthians 5:17 (ESV)
Therefore, if anyone is in Christ, he is a new creation. The old has passed away; behold, the new has come.

2 Corinthians 1:3-4 (NIV)
Praise be to the God and Father of our Lord Jesus Christ, the Father of compassion and the God of all comfort, [4]who comforts us in all our troubles, so that we can comfort those in any trouble with the comfort we ourselves receive from God.

Mark 16:15 (NKJV)
And He said to them, "Go into all the world and preach the gospel to every creature.

The Twelve Steps:
Final Thoughts
and Why It Works

"More and more we became interested in seeing
what we could contribute to life. As we felt new
power flow in, as we enjoyed peace of mind, as
we discovered we could face life successfully,
as we became conscious of His presence, we
began to lose our fear of today, tomorrow or the
hereafter. We were reborn."[105]
(Alcoholics Anonymous)

==================================

"Jesus answered and said to him,
"Most assuredly, I say to you, unless one is born
again, he cannot see the kingdom of God."
(John 3:3 NKJV)

==================================

"And yet as we look at the millions of people in
AA and NA fellowships that have been
successful in recovery, we see it works. The
spiritual solution does indeed work."[106]
(The Hope Recovery Devotional)

==================================

This final chapter is called "The Twelve Steps: Final Thoughts and Why It Works". It is clear from reading the Twelve Steps of Recovery from either AA or NA that The Twelve Steps are very much centered on God and having a "spiritual awakening" and ultimately a restored relationship with God. Certainly, The Twelve Steps have helped many millions of people be successful in recovery and it is unmistakable that God and a spiritual relationship with God are key components of why The Twelve Steps have been so successful. With that being the case, I encourage you to not overlook and to not minimize the significance of this God connection and of this spiritual component to the Twelve Steps. But that you seriously consider bringing God into your life and guiding you through these Twelve Steps, ultimately leading you to not only success in recovery, but a "spiritual awakening" and a restored relationship with God as well.

I'd like to suggest four brief points regarding The Twelve Steps of Recovery as my final thoughts of why they work so well. Also, what I see as the main reasons that make it so successful, and why it is so helpful for so many people to be successful in recovery and that also lead to a dramatically changed life.

More Than a Recovery Program
"An amazing spiritual program"

First, it is absolutely true that The Twelve Steps of Recovery are an amazing recovery program, but they are much more than that, they are "an amazing spiritual program" as well. These Twelve Steps bring addicts and alcoholics, and even all of us, face to face with that fact that there is a God in heaven. There is a "higher power", and it is only by having a spiritual experience and a restored relationship with God, that we can really live a full and abundant life. It is a life with true inner peace and joy, such that when we lay our heads down at night, we have a peace and calmness in our mind, body, and spirit. We are no longer tortured by the painful obsession for drugs and alcohol, but we truly have a peace and calmness, and even a joy and happiness in life and it is all because of The Twelve Steps of Recovery and of a "spiritual awakening" and a restored relationship with God.

AA speaks to this dramatic impact of The Twelve Steps as a spiritual program when it says on page 25:

> "The great fact is just this, and nothing less: That we have had deep and effective spiritual experiences* which have revolutionized our whole attitude toward life, toward our fellows and toward God's universe. The central fact of our lives today is the absolute certainty that our Creator has entered into our hearts and lives in a way which is indeed miraculous. He has commenced to accomplish those things for us which we could never do by ourselves."[107]

The Twelve Steps of Recovery are much more than just a recovery program; they are an amazing spiritual program as well. They are a spiritual program that leads to a spiritual awakening, a restored relationship with God, and a full and abundant life as well.

All About Prayer
"Another way to pray"

The Twelve Steps are also all about prayer. It may be The Twelve Steps do not appear at first glance to be about prayer, but as you look closer, they really are very much about prayer, but just "another way to pray". Several of the steps talk about prayer in new and different ways, but they are still very much about prayer, such as, 'we made a decision, we admitted to God, we humbly asked Him, we sought through prayer and meditation.' All of these indicate prayer. They indicate prayer to God for help in recovery, for help with relationships, and help in life. Many people will often say several of the steps as prayers every day praying Step Three, Step Seven and Step Eleven and even other steps and other prayers as well.

In many ways the prayers and guidance of The Twelve Steps are quite consistent with the Lord's Prayer as given in Matthew 6:9-13 (NKJV) when the Lord teaches us to pray as:

"Our Father in heaven, Hallowed be Your name. [10] Your kingdom come. Your will be done On earth as *it is* in heaven. [11] Give us this day our daily bread. [12] And forgive us our debts, As we forgive our debtors. [13] And do not lead us into temptation, But deliver us from the evil one. For Yours is the kingdom and the power and the glory forever. Amen."

The Lord's Prayer and Step Eleven are both very similar, as they both focus on God's will in our life. Step Eleven says:

"We sought through prayer and meditation to improve our conscious contact with God as we understood him, praying only for knowledge of his will for us and the power to carry that out."[108]

All About Helping Others
"Helping those still struggling with addiction"

The Twelve Steps are all about helping others and specifically "helping those still struggling with addiction". For those in recovery, giving back and helping others is the best defense against relapse or put another way giving back is the best 'insurance' against relapse. NA speaks to this when it says on page 50:

"By this time, most of us realize that the only way that we can keep what was given to us is by sharing this new gift of life with the still-suffering addict. This is our best insurance against relapse to the torturous existence of using. We call it carrying the message, and we do it in a number of ways (and later...) We received our recovery from the God of our understanding. We now make ourselves available as His tool to share recovery with those who seek it."[109]

At a recent meeting someone shared that "relapse is not required". You do not have to relapse as a part of your recovery story. I encourage you to embrace the recovery program of The Twelve Steps and to embrace the spiritual program of the Twelve Steps. Do everything necessary to be successful in recovery and leave any relapse in the past, and continue to help others that are still struggling, and that will also be your "best insurance against relapse" as well.

The Steps Do Not Stop
"They are a new way of living"

The Twelve Steps of Recovery do not stop. "They are a new way of living". You are never really done with The Twelve Steps, as Step Twelve says "to practice these principles in all our affairs". The Twelve Steps are an amazing recovery program and an amazing spiritual program as well, and for me, that is the main reason that it is so successful and how they are able to help so many people to be successful in recovery and to lead dramatically changed lives. The Twelve Steps point people to God and to a spiritual relationship with God. As you work The Twelve Steps of Recovery, you can grow in your recovery, and that is the most important thing, because if you are not successful in recovery, everything else falls apart. And as you continue to work the steps, you will not only grow in your recovery, but you will grow in your faith and in your spiritual relationship with God, and that is where a full and abundant life comes in, as you grow with God.

I encourage you to continue moving forward in your recovery and to continue to work The Twelve Steps of Recovery as a key part of your recovery and as a key part of your spiritual relationship with God as well.

As I close this last chapter, I encourage you to consider The Twelve Steps as much more than just a recovery program, but as a spiritual program as well. Also, I ask you to consider these Twelve Steps for you personally and for you to consider what you truly believe about God and what you believe about a "higher power" and then consider how your life might be dramatically changed if you bring God into your life. John 3:16 (NIV) beautifully describes the message of the Bible saying:

> "For God so loved the world that he gave his one and only Son, that whoever believes in him shall not perish but have eternal life."

I encourage you to consider that with God in your life, you can be successful in recovery, and even beyond that, you can have a full and abundant life. You can have a life such that when you lay your head down at night, you can have a peace and calmness in your mind and body and spirit. Indeed, success in recovery is possible through a faith-based journey of The Twelve Steps of Recovery.

Brief Summary of
'Final Thoughts and Why It Works'

These four key principles of The Twelve Steps of Recovery, and how they are much more than just a recovery program, are listed as:

1) More Than a Recovery Program
   a. "An amazing spiritual program as well".
2) All About Prayer
   a. "Another way to pray".
3) All About Helping Others
   a. "Helping those still struggling with addiction".
4) The Steps Do Not Stop
   a. "They are a new way of living".

The Twelve Steps of Alcoholics Anonymous

1. We admitted we were powerless over alcohol—that our lives had become unmanageable.

2. Came to believe that a Power greater than ourselves could restore us to sanity.

3. Made a decision to turn our will and our lives over to the care of God *as we understood Him.*

4. Made a searching and fearless moral inventory of ourselves.

5. Admitted to God, to ourselves, and to another human being the exact nature of our wrongs.

6. Were entirely ready to have God remove all these defects of character.

7. Humbly asked Him to remove our shortcomings.

8. Made a list of all persons we had harmed, and became willing to make amends to them all.

9. Made direct amends to such people wherever possible, except when to do so would injure them or others.

10. Continued to take personal inventory and when we were wrong promptly admitted it.

11. Sought through prayer and meditation to improve our conscious contact with God *as we understood Him*, praying only for knowledge of His will for us and the power to carry that out.

12. Having had a spiritual awakening as the result of these steps, we tried to carry this message to alcoholics, and to practice these principles in all our affairs.

The Twelve Steps of
Narcotics Anonymous

1. We admitted that we were powerless over our addiction, that our lives had become unmanageable.

2. We came to believe that a Power greater than ourselves could restore us to sanity.

3. We made a decision to turn our will and our lives over to the care of God as we understood Him.

4. We made a searching and fearless moral inventory of ourselves.

5. We admitted to God, to ourselves, and to another human being the exact nature of our wrongs.

6. We were entirely ready to have God remove all these defects of character.

7. We humbly asked Him to remove our shortcomings.

8. We made a list of all persons we had harmed, and became willing to make amends to them all.

9. We made direct amends to such people wherever possible, except when to do so would injure them or others.

10. We continued to take personal inventory and when we were wrong promptly admitted it.

11. We sought through prayer and meditation to improve our conscious contact with God as we understood Him, praying only for knowledge of His will for us and the power to carry that out.

12. Having had a spiritual awakening as a result of these steps, we tried to carry this message to addicts, and to practice these principles in all our affairs.

Thank you for supporting the faith-based recovery resources of www.HopeRecovery.us. Please consider making these and other faith-based recovery resources available for churches, recovery ministries, recovery facilities, or recovery groups to provide even more options for people to be successful in recovery.

Other faith-based recovery books available are:

The Hope Recovery Devotional:
There is Always Hope With God

The Twelve Keys of Faith-Based Recovery:
How to Be Successful in Recovery
By Embracing Key Biblical Truths

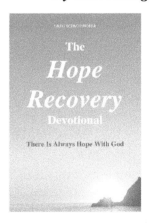 

Footnotes

[1] Bill W., Alcoholics Anonymous. 2nd ed. (New York City NY, Alcoholics Anonymous World Services, Inc., 1955), 55.

[2] Greg Schmalhofer, The Hope Recovery Devotional: There is Always Hope with God, Large Print Ed. (Schmalhofer,2023), 212.

[3] Narcotics Anonymous, 6th ed. (Van Nuys, CA, Narcotics Anonymous World Services, Inc., 2008), xxv.

[4] Bill W., Alcoholics Anonymous, 12.

[5] Narcotics Anonymous, 6th ed. , 25.

[6] Narcotics Anonymous, 6th ed. , 17.

[7] Narcotics Anonymous, 6th ed. , 17.

[8] Schmalhofer, The Hope Recovery Devotional, LP Ed., 93.

[9] Narcotics Anonymous, 6th ed. , 17.

[10] Narcotics Anonymous, 6th ed. , 20.

[11] Bill W., Alcoholics Anonymous, 58.

[12] Narcotics Anonymous, 6th ed. , 21.

[13] Bill W., Alcoholics Anonymous, 25.

[14] Narcotics Anonymous, 6th ed. , 17.

[15] Narcotics Anonymous, 6th ed. , 17.

[16] Schmalhofer, The Hope Recovery Devotional, LP Ed., 94.

[17] Narcotics Anonymous, 6th ed. , 17.

[18] Narcotics Anonymous, 6th ed. , 17.

[19] Bill W., Alcoholics Anonymous, 45.

[20] Narcotics Anonymous, 6th ed. , 17.

[21] Narcotics Anonymous, 6th ed. , 17.

[22] Narcotics Anonymous, 6th ed. , 17.

[23] Schmalhofer, The Hope Recovery Devotional, LP Ed., 97.

[24] Narcotics Anonymous, 6th ed. , 17.

[25] Bill W., Alcoholics Anonymous, 62.

[26] Narcotics Anonymous, 6th ed. , 25.

[27] Narcotics Anonymous, 6th ed. , 17.

[28] Narcotics Anonymous, 6th ed. , 17.

[29] Schmalhofer, The Hope Recovery Devotional, LP Ed., 99.

[30] Bill W., Alcoholics Anonymous, 63.

[31] Narcotics Anonymous, 6th ed. , 17.

[32] Bill W., Alcoholics Anonymous, 64.

[33] Narcotics Anonymous, 6th ed. , 30.

[34] Narcotics Anonymous, 6th ed. , 27.

[35] Narcotics Anonymous, 6th ed. , 29.

[36] Narcotics Anonymous, 6th ed. , 30.

[37] Narcotics Anonymous, 6th ed. , 17.

[38] Narcotics Anonymous, 6th ed. , 17.

[39] Schmalhofer, The Hope Recovery Devotional, LP Ed., 100.

[40] Narcotics Anonymous, 6th ed. , 17.

[41] Bill W., Alcoholics Anonymous, 72.

[42] Narcotics Anonymous, 6th ed., 31.

[43] Narcotics Anonymous, 6th ed. , 31.

[44] Bill W., Alcoholics Anonymous, 75.

[45] Narcotics Anonymous, 6th ed. , 17.

[46] Narcotics Anonymous, 6th ed. , 33.

[47] Narcotics Anonymous, 6th ed. , 17.

[48] Narcotics Anonymous, 6th ed. , 17.

[49] Schmalhofer, The Hope Recovery Devotional, LP Ed., 102.

[50] Narcotics Anonymous, 6th ed. , 17.

[51] Narcotics Anonymous, 6th ed. , 34.

[52] Narcotics Anonymous, 6th ed. , 34.

[53] Narcotics Anonymous, 6th ed. , 17.

[54] Spiritual Kindergarten: Christian Perspectives on the Twelve Steps, (Brea, CA, Christian Recovery international, 2008),48-49.

[55] Narcotics Anonymous, 6th ed. , 346.

[56] Narcotics Anonymous, 6th ed. , 17.

[57] Narcotics Anonymous, 6th ed. , 17.

[58] Schmalhofer, The Hope Recovery Devotional, LP Ed., 104.

[59] Narcotics Anonymous, 6th ed. , 17.

[60] Narcotics Anonymous, 6th ed. , 17.

[61] Narcotics Anonymous, 6th ed. , 36.

[62] Narcotics Anonymous, 6th ed. , 36.

[63] Narcotics Anonymous, 6th ed. , 17.

[64] Narcotics Anonymous, 6th ed. , 36.

[65] Narcotics Anonymous, 6th ed. , 17.

[66] Narcotics Anonymous, 6th ed. , 17.

[67] Schmalhofer, The Hope Recovery Devotional, LP Ed., 107.

[68] Narcotics Anonymous, 6th ed. , 17.

[69] Narcotics Anonymous, 6th ed. , 39.

[70] Bill W., Alcoholics Anonymous, 77.

[71] Narcotics Anonymous, 6th ed. , 38.

[72] Narcotics Anonymous, 6th ed. , 17.

[73] Narcotics Anonymous, 6th ed. , 17.

[74] Narcotics Anonymous, 6th ed. , 17.

[75] Schmalhofer, The Hope Recovery Devotional, LP Ed., 108.

[76] Narcotics Anonymous, 6th ed. , 17.

[77] Narcotics Anonymous, 6th ed. , 40.

[78] Narcotics Anonymous, 6th ed. , 41.

[79] Narcotics Anonymous, 6th ed. , 42.

[80] Narcotics Anonymous, 6th ed. , 17.

[81] Narcotics Anonymous, 6th ed. , 17.

[82] Narcotics Anonymous, 6th ed. , 17.

[83] Schmalhofer, The Hope Recovery Devotional, LP Ed., 110.

[84] Narcotics Anonymous, 6th ed. , 17.

[85] Bill W., Alcoholics Anonymous, 84.

[86] Narcotics Anonymous, 6th ed. , 42.

[87] Narcotics Anonymous, 6th ed. , 17.

[88] Narcotics Anonymous, 6th ed. , 17.

[89] Bill W., Alcoholics Anonymous, 85.

[90] Narcotics Anonymous, 6th ed. , 17.

[91] Narcotics Anonymous, 6th ed. , 17.

[92] Schmalhofer, The Hope Recovery Devotional, LP Ed, 112.

[93] Narcotics Anonymous, 6th ed. , 17.

[94] Narcotics Anonymous, 6th ed. , 45.

[95] Bill W., Alcoholics Anonymous, 87.

[96] Narcotics Anonymous, 6th ed. , 17.

[97] Narcotics Anonymous, 6th ed. , 17.

[98] Narcotics Anonymous, 6th ed. , 17.

[99] Schmalhofer, The Hope Recovery Devotional, LP Ed., 115.

[100] Narcotics Anonymous, 6th ed. , 17.

[101] Bill W., Alcoholics Anonymous, 99.

[102] Narcotics Anonymous, 6th ed. , 49.

[103] Narcotics Anonymous, 6th ed. , 17.

[104] Narcotics Anonymous, 6th ed. , 17.

[105] Bill W., Alcoholics Anonymous, 63.

[106] Schmalhofer, The Hope Recovery Devotional, LP Ed., 205.

[107] Bill W., Alcoholics Anonymous, 25.

[108] Narcotics Anonymous, 6th ed. , 17.

[109] Narcotics Anonymous, 6th ed. , 50.